FABRIC APPLIQUÉ FOR WORSHIP

*Patterns and Guide
for Sewing
Banners, Vestments,
and Paraments*

Rebecca Jerdee

Augsburg Publishing House, Minneapolis

CONTENTS

Fabric Appliqué for Worship

Cover design by Koechel/Peterson Design
Inside illustrations by Rebecca Jerde
International Standard Book No. 0-8066-1965-1

Chapter 1

VISUAL COMMUNICATION

Scripture calls us to worship with all of our senses, with our minds, hearts, and hands—seeing, hearing, smelling, touching, and tasting. The sounds of music and the reading of the Scriptures, the touch of hands in greeting, the smell of burning incense and candles, the taste of bread and wine—all of these involve us in the worship of our God.

Our sight also involves us in worship. By our sight we perceive some of the direct messages. Seeing the congregation gathered together reminds us of our membership in the whole family of God. Seeing a cross recalls the death and resurrection of Jesus. Seeing the baptismal water as it splashes over the baptized tells us that we are made new, cleansed, renewed. Seeing a procession of worshipers waving palm branches recalls that biblical event when Jesus entered Jerusalem. Seeing the bread broken and the wine poured reinforces the knowledge that it was given "for you." These visuals powerfully communicate the gospel in contemporary worship life.

The fabrics that accompany our worship can be significant communication tools too. Combining symbolic image and color, these fabrics lead us to a mood and spirit of worship and to the message of the gospel.

Color both is and can carry a message. The specific colors appointed for the seasons and festivals of the church year are chosen to reveal the central theme of that day or time. The use of color in the worship space also contributes to the mood and spirit of worship. A good symbol points to that which is beyond sight, that which draws us to God. As contemporary Christians, we borrow our ideas for symbols from nature or from objects within our human experience. By attaching stories and meanings to the symbols, we make expressions of the unexplainable mysteries of God. The combination of color and symbol in the fabrics of worship can powerfully communicate the gospel and a mood for worship.

In an earlier time of slow-paced industry, loving hands produced hand-woven and hand-embroidered fabrics for the church. By today's measures, such laborious hours spent on liturgical arts are extravagant, almost impossible to buy. They were expensive for the early church, too, but in those times there was no alternative. And the hours spent in painstaking labor became precious offerings.

The industrial age, with its wonderful machines and marvelous efficiency, began to produce ecclesiastical arts with greater ease. Time spent in the production of liturgical cloth decreased dramatically, and the availability increased so that every church was able to dress its altar in exquisite, rich fabrics at relatively little cost.

Fabric appliqué combines the handmade traditions of the past with the industrial innovations of the present. It accomplishes the same graphic storytelling as the hand-embroidered tapestries of early days. The age of machines and computers gives us a great wealth of fabrics from which to choose as well as the versatile zigzag sewing machine, a valuable tool in the hands of a creative person.

This book, designed to help congregations develop fabric appliquéd worship arts, is a resource for worship planning committees, a source for liturgical designs for the church year, an instructional handbook for stitching the paraments and vestments, and a springboard for congregations who design their own church arts. For beginners, parament and vestment designs with step-by-step instructions are included. While the instructions are specific, the projects are easily personalized for a congregation simply by changing the symbols or sizes suggested. The projects are intended to be flexible, adaptable to the particular congregation.

Once the basic appliqué techniques have been mastered, the designs and patterns can be adapted to create new designs that are especially meaningful to the congregation's worship life.

Chapter 2

PRELIMINARY EVALUATION

Stitching fabric appliqué for worship can be as simple as sewing a strip of sheepskin to a piece of tanned leather or as complex as combining 100 pieces of appliquéd patches of fabric in an elaborate display of color and symbol. But, however you approach the visual elements of the worship setting for your congregation, the work can be challenging, exciting, and spiritually nourishing.

Begin by planning. You will be making visual arts for a community of believers rather than for your own personal use, so include a number of people in your preliminary planning. With a worship or music and arts committee or an altar guild, you might briefly describe the general character and attitude of the congregation, outline its limitations and resources for handling visual arts projects, and consider specific needs for particular visuals.

To get started on this stitching adventure, define your congregation's visual worship needs. Use the following questions and suggestions as you begin your journey through the Scriptures in a search for meaningful worship arts ideas.

The Congregation's Identity

Describe the general characteristics of your congregation. What occupations, educations, skills, and talents do its members possess? What type of community does it serve? What is unique about your congregation?

Describe your congregation's special interests. Are members musical, youth-oriented, educational, or mission conscious? Does the congregation actively pursue evangelism, social action, community involvement, or ecumenism? What symbols has the congregation adopted that indicate its special interests?

Describe the congregation's history. How old is it? What changes has it experienced in terms of size, location, or buildings? Does it celebrate its anniversary, name saint, or special days that other congregations do not?

Describe the present status of the congregation. What are the general characteristics and attitudes of the clergy and laity toward worship? What is its present financial situation? What is the state of the present building, the condition of the worship center? How ready is the congregation for visual change?

The Congregation's Resources

Consider the limitations of the building, its present visual arts. How much space is available for decoration? What space should not be decorated? What is the condition of the paraments, vestments, and banners? What storage is available for cloths and banners when they are not in use? Which visual arts are now useless, inferior, old or worn, no longer meaningful to the life of the church?

Consider the resources provided by your church's membership. What emphasis does the clergy make in the worship life of your congregation? What counsel does the pastor offer? Are there designers cr artists in your membership to provide leadership in the selection of fabrics, symbols, and other visual appointments? Does your congregation hire outside help for the designing and making of its paraments, vestments, and banners? Do members show enthusiasm for the making of decorations by hand? Are there seamstresses or tailors? Are members of the congregation skilled in other handcrafts?

What funds are provided by the congregation for the visual arts? What financial resources could be tapped for funding future projects?

Consider outside sources. What resources in your community are available to help your congregation with its visual arts? What books, pamphlets, and other printed materials are available for ideas? What ecclesiastical arts companies should be considered?

The Congregation's Worship
THE SACRAMENTS

How often does your congregation celebrate Holy Baptism? Does your congregation present a stitched baptismal bib or white poncho-like garment to the baptized during the ceremony? What kind of gifts does the congregation give to the baptismal candidates?

Does the pastor wear a chasuble at the celebration of Holy Communion? Is the altar always covered with a cloth? What could be placed in the narthex of the church to announce Holy Baptism or Holy Communion at that day's service?

THE CHURCH YEAR

The Advent Season. Will blue or purple paraments be placed on the altar for Advent? Does the pastor have blue or purple vestments? Could you hang a banner that builds Sunday by Sunday during the four Sundays in Advent? Do you use the Advent wreath as part of your tradition? How could you "prepare the way of the Lord" in a new way this year? Are Christmas decorations, parties, and music reserved for the 12 days of Christmas to allow Advent symbols their greatest effectiveness and impact? Which scriptures for the four Sundays of Advent suggest symbols for your congregation's use? How could you express the Advent theme of hope, for example?

The Christmas Season. What symbols do the white paraments carry? Could the Christmas paraments and vestments be different than those for Easter? How do you express the "light" theme of the Christmas season? How do you decorate the church during the 12 days of Christmas? How do you decorate the Christmas tree? Does the congregation have a traditional banner or decoration for The Nativity of Our Lord? Does the Sunday school need visual arts to highlight its program? What processional banners are needed?

The Epiphany Season. Could you make a processional banner for Epiphany highlighting the magi and God's people who move toward the star? How is the "light" theme expressed? How is the Holy Spirit pictured on The Baptism of Our Lord? What sun, light, gladness, righteousness symbols appear on The Transfiguration of Our Lord? Could you simplify the worship setting to help worshipers focus on one main idea each Sunday?

What symbols indicate the teachings of Christ during this season? What about developing several pulpit cloths that coincide with the texts for the day? If you were to symbolize the lessons each Sunday with fabric alone, which types of fabric would you hang from the pulpit, lectern, or altar for each Sunday after the Epiphany? How could you illustrate the season's theme of vigorous spiritual growth?

The Lenten Season. Are the paraments for Lent purple or unbleached muslin? Are they without ornamentation, in keeping with the somber theme of the season? Will you use black paraments for

Ash Wednesday? What decorations can be covered or removed from the worship setting in keeping with the contemplative mood of the season? How can you de-emphasize the church's fixtures, cut down on distracting elements?

Holy Week. Do you incorporate the deep red (scarlet) color of Holy Week to change the mood to deeper intensity? Could you use reversible Lenten cloths—purple on one side and deep red on the other? Or could you use layers of cloth to create the change in mood? What passion symbols appear in the worship setting during Holy Week? How could you use palms? Will you strip the altar on Maundy Thursday? How could you use the cross symbol during Holy Week, on Good Friday?

The Easter Season. Will you highlight the Vigil of Easter with visual arts? Or will you choose to let the actual elements of fire, lighted candles, evergreen boughs, water, bread, and wine provide the visual symbols for the evening? Would stitched banners add to or detract from the service?

Will there be a processional with banners on Easter Day? How could you add gold to the white paraments to "crown" the altar, pulpit, and lectern? What flowers, plants, banners, and colors could adorn the church for Easter? What festive decorations could remain for the 50 days of rejoicing to keep the Easter spirit alive through The Day of Pentecost?

The Season after Pentecost. Would a set of deeper green paraments or vestments, in addition to those presently used, indicate a maturing of Christian growth? What fruits or gifts of the Spirit could appear? Could you change decorations several times during the season to freshen and waken the worshiper to new ideas, new growth? What symbols develop from your congregation's experience that are unique to its worship life?

OCCASIONAL SERVICES

What special occasions does your congregation enjoy that come outside of the church calendar year: congregational anniversary, name saint day, mission emphasis, stewardship drive? How could you enrich these special occasions with visual arts? What signals could you send out to the worshiping community?

Does a marriage in the church enjoy special attention from the congregation through a wedding banner? Are births, confirmations, marriages, and deaths recorded on banners?

Once you find a direction you think you should take, contact those in your congregation who are responsible for these decisions: the church council, pastors, designers, and craftspeople.

Chapter 3

BASIC INSTRUCTION

Patterns

SIZING TECHNIQUES

Whether you have designs of your own or plan to use designs from this book, you will need to make patterns for use when cutting the designs from fabrics. You may need to enlarge or reduce original drawings to make the patterns. To complete some of the projects in this book, you will need to enlarge the designs. To accomplish this, choose the method that best suits your needs.

Visual Projection

Opaque Projector. The simplest device for enlargement is the opaque projector. Slide the design under its lens and project the image on a wall at the desired size. Tape large butcher paper to the wall and then draw the image on the paper. The drawing becomes your master pattern. Make a copy of the master pattern for a pattern to cut apart when cutting out the fabric appliqué. To keep track of the parts of a complicated design, number all pattern pieces on both the master pattern and the pattern which will be cut apart.

Overhead Projector. Another easy enlargement can be made with the help of an overhead projector. Trace the design onto a transparent sheet of plastic. Project the image on a wall at the desired size. Again, draw two patterns on large paper, one for a master pattern and one for a cutting pattern.

35mm Slide Projector. A close-up lens on a 35mm camera can photograph the designs on slide film. Develop the film and project the slide onto large paper posted on the wall. Trace over the images. To reduce the size of a design, slide the projector closer to the wall, focus, and trace the smaller image.

Pantograph. Another enlarging device is a pantograph, available in art supply stores.

Grid Enlargement

If you have no visual projection equipment, you can enlarge designs using a grid enlargement method. With tracing paper, trace over the selected design. Mark a grid pattern of one-inch squares over the tracing. To make a pattern twice as big as the traced design, mark a grid pattern of two-inch squares on a large sheet of paper. This grid should contain the same number of squares as the original grid. Transfer the design from the squares on the small grid to the corresponding squares on the larger grid.

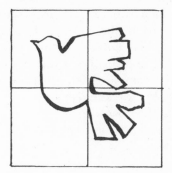

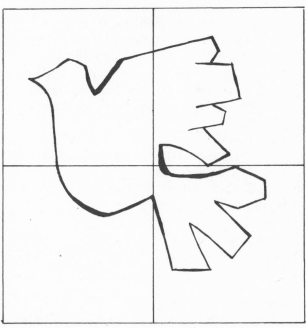

If you wish to use a design from this book in the same proportion as the illustrated vestments, paraments, and banners, check the notations at the bottom of the pattern for the size to make the squares in a grid. For example, if a notation reads *1 square = 4 inches*, make four-inch squares on the large grid and transfer the small drawing from the book onto the large grid.

BASIC PATTERNS

Vestments

Vestments are distinctive garments worn by ministers during worship services. Appliqué patterns for two types of vestments—chasubles and stoles—are given.

Basic garment patterns for chasubles and stoles are shown here. The specific designs in the following chapters will refer back to these basic patterns.

To make the vestment patterns, lay large sheets of newsprint on top of a dressmaker's cutting board that is marked in one-inch squares. Enlarge the drawings as specified, using the cutting board underneath as a guide. The cutting board also helps to establish straight lines in the vestments.

When the patterns are complete, cut them out and use them as you would a dressmaker's pattern. Seam allowances at center back and shoulder seams are 5/8 inches and have been included in the vestment patterns.

Chasubles. A poncho-like garment, the chasuble is worn by the presiding minister during Holy Communion. Patterns for two chasubles are shown here, a short chasuble and a long chasuble.

The yardage for the chasuble patterns follows. This includes fabric for the basic garment only. Fabric for appliqués would be in addition to this.

Long chasuble:
3 1/2 yards fabric, 60 inches wide (without front and back center seams)
or 3 1/2 yards fabric, 52 inches wide (without front and back center seams)

Short chasuble:
3 yards fabric, 45 inches wide (with front and back center seams)

Stoles. Stoles are long, narrow bands of fabric worn around the neck. They are worn by clergy as an indication of ordination. Patterns for two stoles are shown here, a cowled stole and a shaped stole.

The yardage for both stoles is 1 2/3 yards fabric, 45 inches wide. This includes fabric for the basic stole only. Fabric for appliqués would be in addition to this.

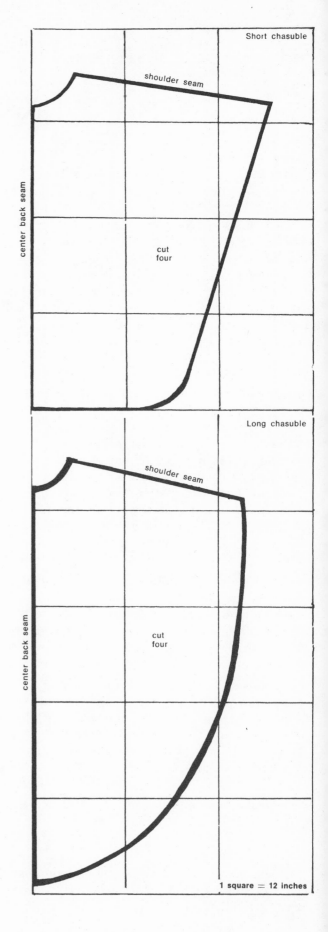

Short chasuble

shoulder seam

center back seam

cut four

Long chasuble

shoulder seam

center back seam

cut four

1 square = 12 inches

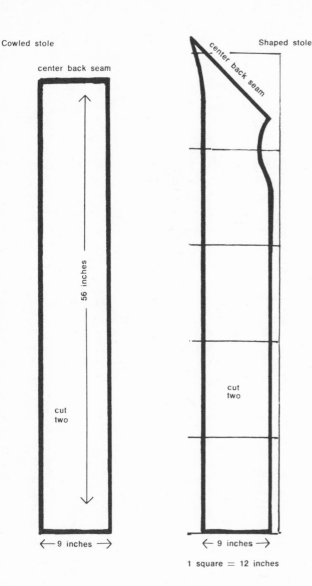

Cowled stole

center back seam

56 inches

cut two

← 9 inches →

Shaped stole

center back seam

cut two

← 9 inches →

1 square = 12 inches

Banners

The dimensions of banners will be somewhat dependent on their use and the space within the sanctuary. Processional banners must be easily carried. Banners hung on the wall must fit the wall space available. You must determine the appropriate size after deciding on the banner's use and place. Processional banner patterns can easily be adapted for wall banners, and vice versa.

Many designs in this book are designated for paraments or vestments. However, most of these designs can easily be translated into banner designs—by enlarging, expanding, multiplying. This is an opportunity for imagination and creativity. A stole design, for example, might be enlarged into a long, thin banner. An altar cloth design might make a marvelous processional banner.

To make a banner pattern, first determine the size of the banner you wish to make. Then, cut newsprint paper to that size. Tack the paper to the wall and project the design you have chosen onto the newsprint. Pull the projector back and forth until you come to a composition that pleases you. You might prefer a large design that exceeds the size of the cloth, or you might choose a small symbol set in a lower corner or central position. You might combine symbols or add lettering. The possibilities are endless.

Trace around the projected design, onto the paper with a black marking pen. This will be your master pattern. Make a copy of this master for a pattern to use when cutting out the pieces for the fabric appliqué.

APPLIQUÉ PATTERNS

Symbols

Many designs in this book require symbols to be appliquéd. In most cases, a symbol pattern is supplied, which must be enlarged. See *Sizing Techniques* for instructions.

Letters

Some of the designs require letters to be appliquéd. A quick and easy way to make letters for appliqués is to slip a transparent sheet of dry transfer lettering onto an overhead projector. The letters can be projected at any desired size onto a paper posted on the wall. These sheets of lettering are available in many different letter styles at office supply stores.

Paraments

Paraments are cloths which adorn chancel furnishings. Designs for altar, pulpit, and lectern cloths are given.

Paraments are made up of two parts—*depth* and *drop* are the terms used to describe those parts in this book. The *drop* is that section of the cloth which hangs down in front of the altar, pulpit, or lectern. This is the part that is usually decorated with appliqué. The *depth* is that part which lies over the top of the altar or over the bookrest of the pulpit or lectern. Often, directions are given and fabric is specified for only the drop. You will have to add the depth which fits the chancel furnishings in your church.

You may also need to adapt the dimensions of the cloths to fit your chancel furnishings. This is especially true of the altar cloth, since the width, height, and length of altars vary greatly.

Choosing Fabrics

The next step is the selection of materials from which to cut and stitch the designs. This can be the most exciting part of the fabric appliqué process because it is your chance to create moods, coordinate colors, choose textures, and experiment with variety.

For some projects you may prefer fine fabrics—white satins, pale taffetas, brocades, chiffons, and laces. Another project might suggest the practical nature of woolens, knits, and corduroys. A third project might best employ leather, sheepskin, drapery weaves, hand-loomed cloths, linens, furs, or felt.

Not only are the choices in color and texture abundant, but modern technology assures that fabrics offer colorfastness and easy care. You can safely combine a variety of fabrics without the disappointment of shrinkage or stretching once the stitched pieces have been washed or dry cleaned.

An imaginative congregation can create paraments, vestments, and banners from a wide variety of materials. For example, the cloths for festivals related to the *work* of the church could be cut from fabrics that suggest work, fabrics made from the stuff of the earth—those made from cotton plants, flax, sheep's wool, jute, or hemp. The fabrics would not only be durable, serviceable, and practical for the long Season after Pentecost, but would suggest the same characteristics of the workers of Christ's church: honest, common, available, practical, and hard-working. These sturdily woven, relatively inexpensive, useful fabrics are the burlaps, sportswears, broadcloths, corduroys, wools, and drapery and upholstery fabrics. Although plain, the fabrics can be of high quality, as finely made as the fabrics of royalty, and eminently suitable for the worship center.

Lent, too, is a good season for fabrics denoting the earthy, humble, common, and plain. A time for reflection and repentance, this season suggests unbleached muslins, monks' cloth, and plain weaves that do not distract by decoration. Humble and practical, these fabrics—often used for sackings and wrappings—remind us of grave cloths and swaddling clothes. They suggest Christ's humanity at the time of his passion and death as well as the clothes of the penitent.

The fair linen, among the plainer fabrics, is a truly beautiful cloth, appropriate for the table of the Lord. One of the oldest woven fabrics, linen has endured through centuries as one of the most respected materials. When laid on the altar, it reminds us of the humility, simplicity, and humanity of Jesus' life on earth.

Pentecost and Advent could combine fabrics of high contrast. These celebrations in which heaven and earth blend, manifest a heavenly child born to a simple woman of the earth and the Holy Spirit alighting on the heads of Christ's followers. What an opportunity for the blending of earthy fabrics with those that suggest the radiance of heaven! Picture fabrics of satiny sheen, smooth in texture, next to the nap of deep corduroys or velveteens. The working fabrics—while inexpensive, washable, and practical—take on a richness and radiance when adjacent to lustrous, shiny fabrics. You could stitch together compositions of metallic and felt fabrics, or combine all four—satin, metallic, felt, and velveteen!

The congregation which experiments with a variety of fabrics for the worship center reserves the most precious fabrics for its highest festivals. The most precious fabric today is handwoven cloth. With time for handwork at a premium, handmade fabric is more treasured than ever. If fine handwoven cloth is not available, you might choose from among the most prized machine-made cloths: Satins offer luster and glow; sheers denote fineness. Gold threads, plush velvets, silk, and linen indicate elegance and value.

Select the fabrics for the design you plan to execute based on the church season it will serve, the technique you will use (machine or hand appliqué), and the care it will be given (washing or dry cleaning). Be sure the fabrics are compatible with each other, easy to cut and stitch together. Choose compatible interfacings and linings.

Always prepare washable fabrics by preshrinking them and by straightening the grain of the fabric. Also, consider the use of the garment or cloth and your climate. For example, when making a chasuble, consider the weight of the fabric and the comfort and ease it will allow its wearer. A cumbersome vestment inhibits the pastor's movement and gestures. Also, warmer climates require cool vestments, while a winter wool fabric might be very comfortable in more temperate zones.

Basic Appliqué Techniques

Although several methods for appliqué are useful, most of the projects in this book require the use of the zigzag sewing machine for application of symbols to vestments, paraments, and banners. These step-by-step procedures should be followed:

PREPARATION

First, patterns must be made. If a chasuble or stole is to be made, the basic garment patterns must be prepared (page 8). Patterns for the symbols and/or letters to be appliquéd must also be sized (page 7).

Washable fabrics must be preshrunk.

CUTTING

Use a clean, sharp scissors.

Cut the basic garment or cloth fabric to the appropriate size and shape.

To cut the pieces for the appliqué, place the larger appliqué pattern pieces straight on the grain

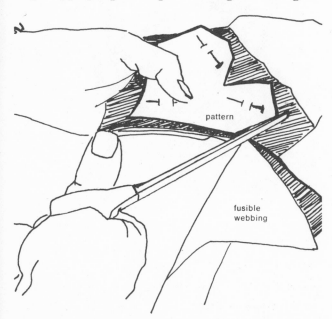

of the fabric. Pin the paper pattern to the fabric as you would for clothing construction. Cut the pieces exactly the shape of the paper pattern. You need not add seam allowances. Smaller shapes that are to be positioned on the background fabric with fusible webbing can be cut off grain, if necessary. Pin the pattern, the fabric, and the fusible webbing together in three layers, and cut all at once.

Many of the projects have appliqués made up of several layers of fabric as well as some over-lapping shapes. Your approach to cutting may vary from project to project. But in most cases you will find it best to cut the larger shapes first and then the smaller ones. You will find more specific cutting instructions included in the directions for each project.

If you want to use a sheer or fine fabric for appliqué but find that it is not easily stitched onto a background fabric, reinforce the finer fabrics with an iron-on interfacing before cutting out the shapes.

CONSTRUCTION

If a loose-woven fabric is selected for the basic garment or cloth, run a line of machine stay stitching along the raw edges of the fabric to prohibit stretching or raveling.

Positioning Appliqués

There are several ways to position the cut shapes on the background fabric before the final appliqué stitching. Use the method that best suits your needs. You may want to combine two or three of the following methods to complete a complicated design.

1. Pin the appliqués to the background fabric and hand baste the layers with a running stitch. This method is suitable especially for large pieces.

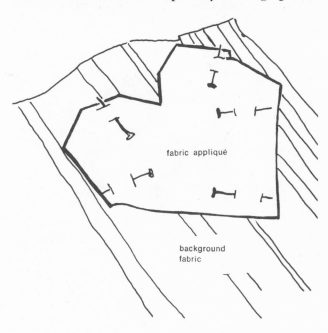

2. Machine baste the layers together with a short, straight stitch or a medium-long, medium-wide, zigzag stitch.

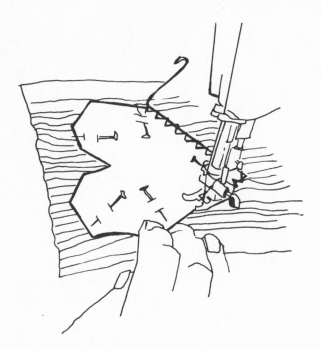

To machine appliqué, set the zigzag machine for a medium-wide satin stitch. Experiment with several machine settings until you find the most satisfactory one. A good setting will flow easily under the foot of the machine. Guide the shapes under the presser foot, neither pushing nor pulling the fabrics, but letting the machine do the work. Satin stitch the appliqué along all raw edges. To stitch around a sharp corner, zigzag up to the corner, leaving the needle in the fabric at the outside of the stitching line. Then, lifting the presser foot and pivoting the fabric, manually turn the wheel on your machine to position the needle on the inside of the stitching line. Lower the presser foot and continue stitching. Modify this procedure to accomplish curves and slight changes in the stitching line.

3. Fuse appliqués to background with fusible webbing or fabric glue, following the instructions that come with the product. Fusible webbing should be used only with small shapes because large pieces shrink and pucker during the fusing process. When using fusible webbing, lay a paper towel over the appliqué before pressing it with the iron. Stray edges of the webbing that stick may cause a build-up on your iron. The paper towel absorbs the stickiness. Use a fresh towel every three fusings.

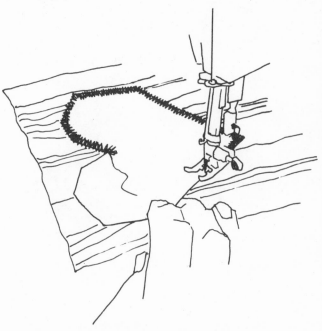

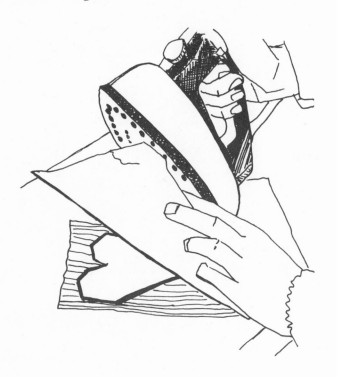

Stitch as much as possible on the appliqué itself before applying it to the basic background fabric, since smaller pieces are easier to maneuver through the machine than larger ones. This also prevents a build-up of stitches that might cause puckering on the background fabrics. When the stitching is finished, pull threads through the back of the appliquéd fabric and tie them off. Press the vestment, parament, or banner on the back side to straighten and to set stitches.

If there seems to be shrinking or pulling of the background fabric behind the appliqué, relieve the tension by cutting out the background fabric behind the appliqué.

Hand Appliqué

Another practical and durable method, appliquéing by hand, has served well for centuries and only recently has been alternated with the machine appliqué method.

To cut pattern pieces for hand appliqué, add ½-inch seam allowances along the outside edges to allow for turning raw edges under. First, pin the appliqué to the background fabric. Turn the seam allowances under, clipping corners and curves along seam allowances to allow easy turning. Baste by hand with a running stitch. Sometimes

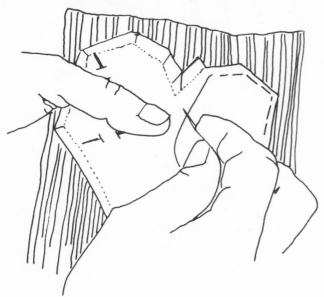

pinning is sufficient "basting" to position the piece for the final stitching.

To finish the appliqué, stitch the folded edge to the background with a whipstitch.

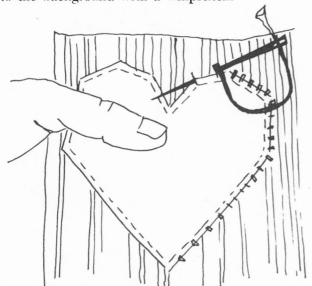

Appliqué Embellishment

Explore ways to add detail to the appliqué work. When design pieces are chunky and large, they can be trimmed, embellished, and highlighted by small details. The contrast of large and small shapes enriches the design, giving it eye appeal. Some practical ways to add details to machine or hand appliqué work follow.

1. Create a narrow line along the edges of shapes by machine couching. Fasten a six-strand line of embroidery floss to the appliqué with a loose, narrow zigzag stitch.

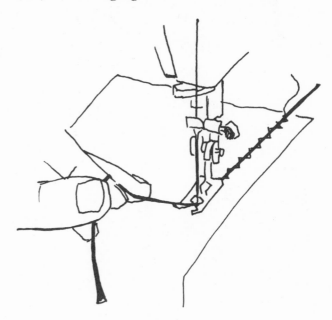

2. Use the decorative stitches that are built into your zigzag sewing machine.

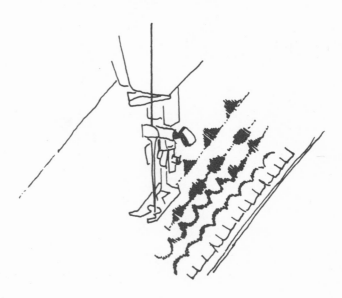

3. Use hand embroidery stitches. Couched threads and running and stem stitches make good lines. The satin stitch fills in shapes, while the buttonhole and whipstitches are excellent for edging shapes with borders to highlight the colors of the symbol.

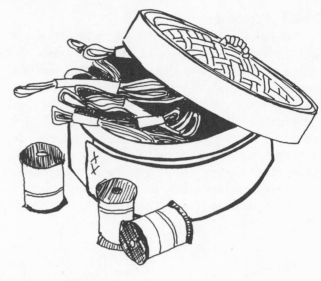

Couched thread

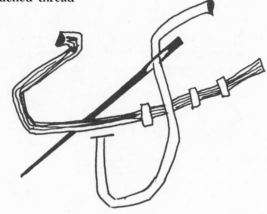

Stem stitch

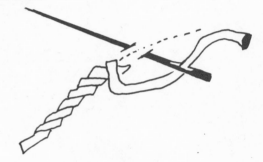

Satin stitch

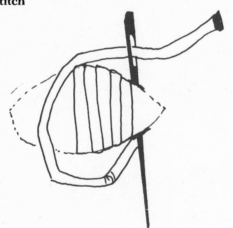

Buttonhole stitch

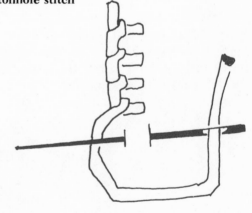

Whipstitch

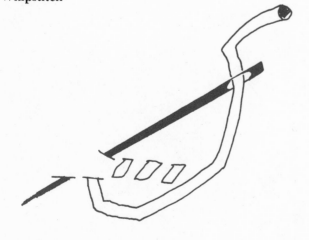

Running stitch

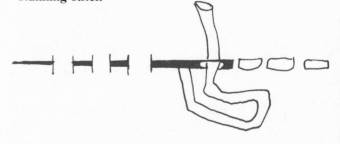

Finishing

Finally, after the appliqué is completed, the garments must be sewed together, interfaced, and lined.

Vestments. The stole is not put together until the two sides have been appliquéd and embellished. Stitch the center back seam using a 5/8-inch seam allowance. Appliqué a symbol across the center seam on the stole back, if desired. Roll the side edges toward the back 1 1/2 inches and press them before interfacing and lining the stole.

To construct the chasuble, sew up the center back and center front seams. Appliqué symbols to the front and/or back, then sew the shoulder seams. The chasuble may be hemmed around the bottom with a blind-stitch or rolled hem, or it may be bound with bias tape. A lined chasuble needs no hemming.

Paraments. Construct paraments the same as stoles, first decorating the panels with appliqués before interfacing and lining. The main difference between parament and stole construction is that you add the depth pieces of fabric to suspend the paraments in front of the altar, pulpit, or lectern. Use the construction necessary for the furniture in your church. Most altars, pulpits, and lecterns are fitted with small rods, dowels, or curtain rods. Channels are stitched at the ends of the depth, and the rods pass through these channels.

Banners. Banner construction varies. If a banner is made from felt, there is little or no construction to be done. There may be a hem at the bottom and a rod channel at the top. In banners stitched from woven fabrics, side edges must be hemmed before finishing the hems and rod channels. Sculptural banner construction is unique to each project.

Interfacing

It is best to interface every stole, especially those made from lightweight fabrics. Cut the interfacing using the stole pattern, then sew up the center back seam. Pin the interfacing inside the stole at the center back. Lay the side strips on the stole and trim away excess interfacing along the edges until the interfacing lies comfortably inside the pressed edges of the stole. Pin or iron the interfacing, depending on the type used.

Interface paraments the same way.

Lining

To line a stole, cut two pieces of lining, using the stole pattern. Sew up the center back seam and

press it open. Lay the lining right side up on the wrong side of the interfaced stole at the center back seam. Pin the three layers together along the center back seam. Lay one half of the stole length along the length of the ironing board. Roll edges of the lining under along the edges of the stole and press. Pin the folded edges together. Whip-stitch or blind stitch the lining to the stole along the folded edges. Repeat for the other half of the stole to complete lining. Fold corners of the hem edge to form a mitered corner before stitching the lining across the bottom.

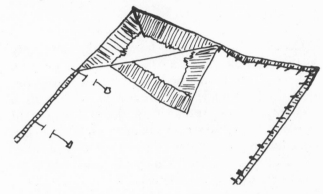

Finish the cowled stole with a length of chain or ribbon stitched at the back of the neck to form the cowl. Fit the stole to its wearer before stitching

the chain in place. The shaped stole sometimes requires a chain at the front fastened at points in the curve of the stole front.

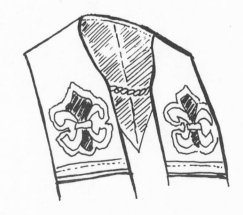

A Velcro fastener stitched inside the back of the neck of a stole and to the pastor's alb or robe keeps the fabric from slipping.

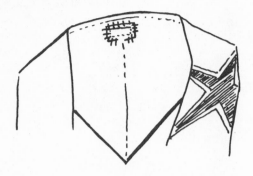

Construct the chasuble lining in the same way as the chasuble. Using a 5/8-inch seam allowance, put the chasuble and the lining right sides together and stitch around the entire hem edge with a straight machine stitch. Turn the chasuble right side out through the neck opening. Finish the neck edge by turning the raw edges in ⅝ inch and either blind stitching or topstitching the edges together. Another way to finish the neck edge is to bind the edges with bias tape.

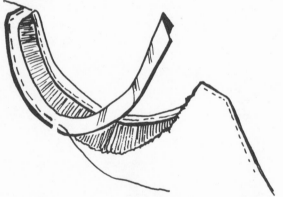

Line paraments the same as stoles, handstitching rolled and pressed edges together on the back side.

A Few Last Words

While we understand that the Lord accepts any offering of heartfelt thanks and praise, we should aspire toward offering him our very best. The fabric work we place in the church should bear excellence in design, execution, function, and effectiveness. Select designs that are neither too simple nor too complex, colors that are neither too dull nor too bright, and fabrics that are neither cheap nor gaudy. Execute the work with your finest craftsmanship to give the cloths their final beauty, grace, and quality, remembering that they are intended to glorify God.

Finally, consider your sewing machine a good friend. As long as you take good care of it, it will do the work. Treat it to a cleaning and oiling after each project as well as a maintenance check at a repair shop at least once a year.

THE CHRISTMAS CYCLE

The Christmas Cycle of the church year—filled with themes of light, joy, and gladness—seems to burst with possibilities for visual symbols and motifs. You might concentrate on the "light" themes suggested in the appointed texts. The following projects designed for Advent, Christmas, and Epiphany draw upon the scripture readings; they are rich with the imagery of stars, lamps, candles, torches, fire, and sun.

The Advent Season

During Advent we anticipate Christ's coming to earth as an infant and as Savior, his coming into the believer's waiting heart today, and his coming again in power and glory. Advent marks the beginning of a new church year, awakening hearts to a new cycle of worship and celebration.

Traditionally, purple—also the color of Lent—adorned church furniture during Advent. But since the characters of the seasons of Advent and Lent are quite different, blue has been specified as an Advent color. By placing blue fabrics on the altar, pulpit, and lectern during Advent, and purple fabrics during Lent, we have an opportunity to define each season with special colors and symbols.

We think of blue as best, as precious. Blue ribbons are best; blue chips, expensive; blue diamonds, rare. For centuries, blue fabrics were cherished and saved for special events. Nature provides very little in the way of permanent dyes for coloring fabrics blue, so weavers of fabrics purchased the expensive indigo plant from the Indies to dye their best cloths with the rich, deep, and durable color. Today we have an abundance of blue dyes synthesized from hydrocarbons, but early churches deemed blue fabrics very precious.

As you begin the church year, your congregation might "prepare the way" in the sanctuary. Clear out all visual elements and start with a fresh look, making the altar the focal point toward which you direct all other visual elements.

STAR OF JACOB ALTAR CLOTHS

"A star shall come forth out of Jacob, and a scepter shall rise out of Israel" (Numbers 24:17).

Your congregation will feel the anticipation of Advent when you hang this four-piece parament on the altar. The excitement of the season builds as you add a section each Sunday in Advent, just as you add a lighted candle to the Advent wreath.

The stars of the heavens remain symbols for us today, just as they did in ancient times. The Star came forth two thousand years ago, his light stretching from the past into the future, leading us from Bethlehem to our time and beyond.

The design for the Advent altar cloth is simple. Half-size star patterns are included. You will trace the star patterns on paper, cut the stars from fabrics and fusible webbing, fuse them in place on

the four blue hangings, machine appliqué, and finish the cloths with interfacings and linings. Tasseled bands laid over the edges of the blue sections highlight the parts.

Size

The finished size of the four combined hangings is 44 x 24 inches, the size including only the drop (the fabric which hangs in front of the altar). The designs were made for an altar measuring 37 x 79 x 28 inches, but they can be adapted to fit any altar.

Materials

3/4 yard deep blue velveteen, 45 inches wide
1 1/2 yards blue lining, 45 inches wide
3/4 yard light blue brushed corduroy, 45 inches wide
1 1/3 yards interfacing, 24 inches wide
1/2 yard light grey satin or millium lining fabric, 45 inches wide
1/2 yard white cotton, 36 inches wide
dark blue, white thread
3 white drapery tassels, 6 inches long
2 packages white satin blanket binding
fusible webbing

Using the five-pointed star pattern, cut five grey satin stars and one deep blue velveteen star. Using the 10-pointed star pattern, cut one white cotton star. Using the circular star pattern, cut 13 white cotton stars. With each star, cut fusible webbing.

Construction. Position the stars on the background fabrics, following the diagram. Fuse them to the background fabric, then machine appliqué raw edges with matching thread. Press the appliqué on the back.

Interface the four cloths, cutting the interfacing 3/4 inch inside the edges of the blue fabric. Fold the edges of the background fabric around the interfacing toward the back of the hanging, and press. If desired, baste the raw edges of the blue velveteen to the interfacing.

Prepare the depth, then stitch them to the drop (the blue sections). Line the four cloths.

To complete the cloth, cut three lengths of satin blanket binding to lay over the edges of the four sections. These strips should be long enough to cover both the drop and the depth of the altar cloth sections. Stitch drapery tassels to the ends of these strips. A strip of white fabric, usually fair

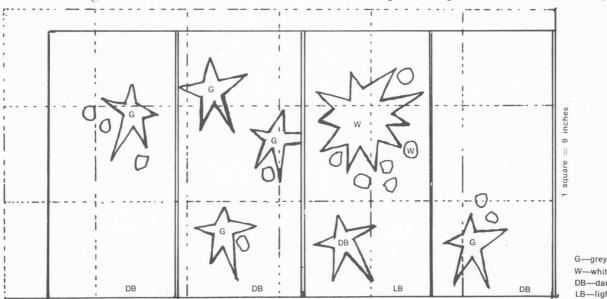

1 square = 9 inches

G—grey
W—white
DB—dark blue
LB—light blue

Directions

Preparation. Enlarge the star patterns to twice their size.

Cutting. Keeping the nap running in one direction, cut three pieces of dark blue velveteen and one piece of light blue brushed corduroy, each measuring 12 1/2 x 26 inches.

linen, can be laid over the depth on top of the altar to secure the four sections and three bands.

Add one piece each Sunday in Advent.

To expand the theme of the altar cloth, you might place complementary cloths on the pulpit and/or lectern. Three designs are given. You might choose to use one, two, or all three, depending on your chancel furnishings.

STAR OF JACOB PULPIT/LECTERN CLOTH

Size

The finished cloth measures 6 x 19 inches and is slightly tapered. This includes only the drop, not the depth.

Materials

This cloth can be made from materials left from the altar cloth project.

Directions

Cutting. Cut the background fabric from the dark blue velveteen fabric, tapering the width of the cloth from six inches (at the top) to eight inches (at the bottom). Using the five-pointed star pattern from the altar cloth, cut one grey satin star, with fusible webbing.

Construction. Fuse the star to the blue background fabric as shown in the illustration. Machine appli-

qué the raw edges with grey thread and press the appliqué on the back.

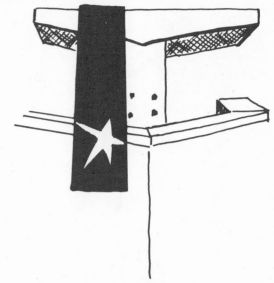

Interface and line the cloth, adding the depth to fit the particular pulpit or lectern.

SCEPTER PULPIT/LECTERN CLOTH

Size

The finished size for the cloth is 14 x 32 inches. This includes both the drop and the depth to fit most standard pulpit or lectern bookrests. Check these dimensions with your chancel furnishings.

Materials

1 piece deep blue velveteen, 16 x 34 inches
*1 yard blue lining fabric, 45 inches wide
1 yard interfacing, 18 inches wide, *or* *1 yard interfacing, 28 inches wide
*1/2 yard white fabric
*1/2 yard fusible webbing
scraps deep blue, light blue, and grey satins and/or corduroys
grey or light blue, dark blue, white thread
*1 skein dark blue six-strand embroidery floss

Directions

Preparation. Enlarge the scepter pattern as specified.

Cutting. Using the pattern, cut the pieces of the design from grey, white, dark blue, and light blue fabrics, each with fusible webbing. Do not cut out

the large white circle. Rather, cut a piece of white fabric approximately 15 inches square. The illustration indicates dark areas for dark blue, shaded areas for light blue or grey, and white areas for white.

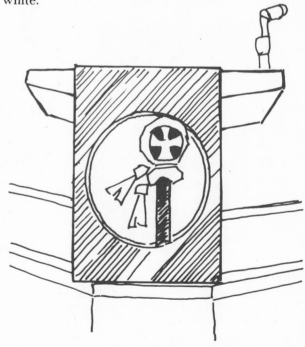

Construction. Fuse the white cross onto the small dark blue circle, then fuse that onto the top shape of the scepter. Fuse all the pieces onto the 15-inch

---

* If both the Scepter and the Messianic Rose pulpit/lectern cloths are made, it is not necessary to duplicate these materials. For example, only one yard of blue lining fabric provides enough material for both cloths.

square piece of white fabric, centered. Next, machine appliqué all raw edges with matching threads, and press on the back side.

Cut the circle with the appliqué out of the white fabric with fusible webbing, following the pattern. Position the circle approximately four inches from the hem edge of the background fabric, centered right to left. Baste it in place, then machine appliqué the raw edge of the circle using white thread.

Machine couch a line of dark blue six-strand embroidery floss on the white fabric, next to the edge of the circle. Press the appliqué on the back side.

Interface and line the cloth, adding the channel or whatever is needed to fit the particular pulpit or lectern.

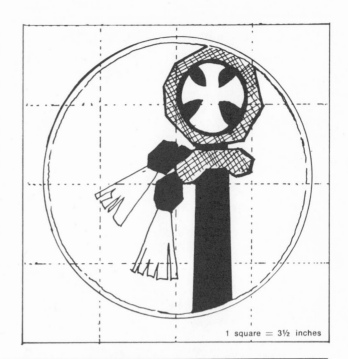

1 square = 3½ inches

MESSIANIC ROSE PULPIT/LECTERN CLOTH

Size

The finished size for the cloth is 14 x 32 inches. This includes both the drop and depth to fit most standard pulpit or lectern bookrests. Check these dimensions with your chancel furnishings.

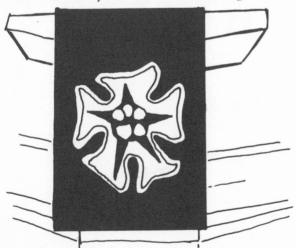

Materials

1 piece light blue brushed corduroy, 16 x 34 inches
° 1 yard blue lining fabric, 45 inches wide
1 yard interfacing, 18 inches wide, *or* ° 1 yard interfacing, 28 inches wide
° 1/2 yard white fabric
° 1/2 yard fusible webbing
scraps of dark blue and green satins and/or corduroys

light blue, dark blue, green, and white thread
° 1 skein dark blue six-strand embroidery floss

Directions

Preparation. Enlarge the rose pattern as specified.

Cutting. Using the pattern, cut out the fabrics: the flower shape from white, the center circle from dark blue, the five points from green, the five seeds

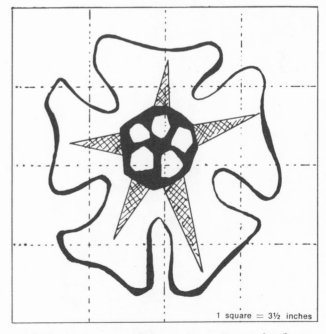

1 square = 3½ inches

° If both the Scepter and the Messianic Rose pulpit/lectern cloths are made, it is not necessary to duplicate these materials. For example, only one yard of blue lining fabric provides enough material for both cloths.

from white. For ease in handling the many pieces, cut the complete center flower shape from the fusible webbing instead of cutting the webbing with each shape. Do cut fusible webbing with each of the seed shapes.

Construction. Position the seed shapes on the blue circle and fuse in place. Center the fusible webbing on the white flower; position the blue circle and the green points on the webbing, and fuse them in place. Next, machine appliqué all raw edges with matching threads.

BLOOMING DESERT CHASUBLE

"The wilderness and the dry land shall be glad, the desert shall rejoice and blossom; like the crocus it shall blossom abundantly, and rejoice with joy and singing" (Isaiah 35:1-2).

To create this spirit of hope, lavish glorious color on the chasuble. You might use a violet-blue woven fabric for the basic chasuble with floral shapes of contrasting colors appliquéd in a rising pyramid arrangement. Some colors are hot, some cool, but all seem intense because of their high

Position the flower on the light blue background fabric approximately four inches from the hem edge, centered right to left, and baste it in place. Machine appliqué the raw edges of the flower with white thread.

Machine couch dark blue, six-strand embroidery floss on the white flower, next to the flower's edge, to highlight the design. Press the appliqué on the back side.

Interface and line the cloth, adding the channel or whatever is necessary to fit the particular pulpit or lectern.

contrasts. Oranges, the natural complement for blue, make up the focal points of the design while the supporting colors are purple, blue, pink, and green. Dark blue bias tape stems and borders tie all the elements together. Because of the bias tape hem on the chasuble, there is no need to line the garment. It is lightweight, easy to wash and wear.

Materials

3 yards violet-blue woven fabric or light sportswear, 45 inches wide
1 1/2 yards fusible webbing, 18 inches wide
1/3 yard each hot pink, purple, pale lavender-blue fabrics
scraps of apricot, pale orange, orange, red-orange, deep blue, and green cottons or broadcloths
orange, pink, lavender, purple, blue, green thread
8 yards dark blue single-fold bias tape

Directions

Preparation. Prepare the short chasuble pattern (page 8). Enlarge the crocus pattern as specified.
Cutting. Using the short chasuble pattern, cut the front and back pieces from the violet-blue fabric.

Using the pattern, cut the crocus shapes, each with fusible webbing. Follow the color key.
Construction. Stitch both the center back and center front seams of the chasuble, using a 5/8-inch seam allowance. Press the seams open.

Position the flower pieces according to the diagram. Center the top crocus on the center seam, 5 1/2 inches from the neck edge. Add two crocuses below it, overlapping the top crocus at the bottom. Repeat this procedure for the third row. Fuse the crocus shapes in place.

Machine appliqué the shapes to the chasuble, changing thread to match the fabric colors. When all the stitching is completed, press the back of the appliqué.

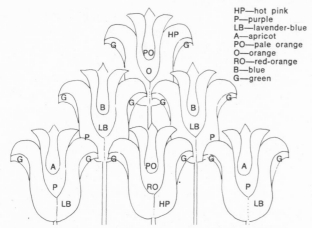

HP—hot pink
P—purple
LB—lavender-blue
A—apricot
PO—pale orange
O—orange
RO—red-orange
B—blue
G—green

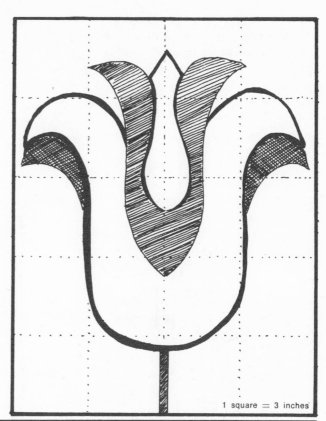

1 square = 3 inches

To make the stems, apply the dark blue bias tape at the base of each flower using a straight machine stitch.

To finish the chasuble, sew the shoulder seams, and press them open. Stitch the bias tape trim to hem and neck edges by placing the right side of the bias trim to the wrong side of the chasuble and stitching 1/4 inch from the edge. Turn the trim to the right side of the chasuble, press, and hand-stitch the remaining folded edge to chasuble.

TREE OF JESSE CHASUBLE

This project transforms the chasuble into a word banner worn by the presiding minister during Holy Communion. The wide, blue spread of the garment recalls the Old Testament promise of the coming Messiah. The chasuble can be appliquéd with the Jesse symbol only, if desired, but the added lettering makes a sparkling, graphic border along the edges of the garment. Old English text type letters were chosen for the chasuble because they suggest ancient scriptures and writings. The text on the chasuble border reads: . . . *from the stump of Jesse, a branch shall grow. Isaiah 11:1.*

Materials

3 yards lightweight blue woven fabric, 45 inches wide
3 yards lining fabric, 45 inches wide
3/4 yard unbleached fabric, 45 inches wide
1/2 yard white broadcloth, 45 inches wide
1/4 yard yellow broadcloth, 36 inches wide
1 yard fusible webbing
white, blue, yellow thread

Directions

Preparation. Prepare the short chasuble pattern (page 8). Enlarge the Jesse Tree pattern to 30 inches high.

Make patterns for the letters on the border (page 9). For this project you need capitals *J* and *I*, and lowercase letters *a, b, c, e, f, g, h, i, l, m, n, o, p, r, s, t, u, w,* the number *1,* a comma, and a period. Enlarge capital letters to five inches high and lower case letters to three inches high.

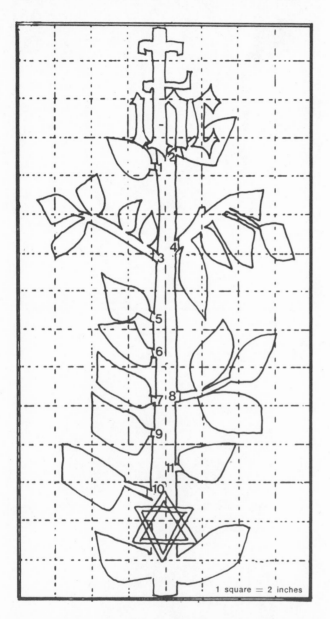

1 square = 2 inches

Cutting. Using the short chasuble pattern, cut the chasuble pieces from the blue woven fabric. Cut the tree stem and *IHS* monogram from unbleached fabric and fusible webbing. Cut 1/2-inch branch stumps along the stem at the places where branches will be added (see the diagram). Number the enlarged pattern at each branch intersection to keep track of the pieces cut away from the pattern when cutting out the tree stem. Cut the branches and leaves from white fabric and fusible webbing. Cut the star of David and the letters for *Jesse* and *Isaiah 11:1* from yellow fabric and fusible webbing.

Cut the letters for the text from white and unbleached fabric. Use your own sense of design for making some words white and others unbleached. The exchange of the two whites gives the appliqué variety and interest. With each letter cut fusible webbing. To spell out the text you will need one *b, c, e, g, n, p, u,* and *w;* two each of *f, l, s, t, m;* three each of *a, h, o,* and *r;* four periods and five commas.

Construction. Stitch both the center back and center front seams of the woven blue chasuble pieces, using a 5/8-inch seam allowance. Press the seams open.

Fuse the stem and the monogram to the center back of the chasuble. Fuse the branches and leaves in place. Machine appliqué all raw edges of the tree, branches, and leaves with white thread.

Fuse the star of David and the letters for *Jesse* to the chasuble back as shown in the illustration. Fuse *Isaiah 11:1* to the chasuble front along the bottom edge, in the center. Machine appliqué around all raw edges with yellow thread. Press the appliqués on the back side.

Stitch the chasuble front to the back at the shoulders, and press the seams open.

Position the rest of the letters according to the illustration. Fuse them in place and machine appliqué with white thread.

Press the chasuble on the back side and then line it.

STAR OF DAVID STOLE

Borrowing the idea of Jesus' lineage from the Tree of Jesse chasuble, you can abbreviate it for a stole design. Make a graphic statement by lettering one side of the stole with *Jesse.* Run a line toward the back of the neck and there stitch the star of David. Continue the line toward the other side of the stole lettered with *Jesus.* Color it in bright blues, yellows, and golds, Winter wool blends woven with a white fleck relate well to the homespun fabric of the clergy's white robe.

Materials
2 pieces blue wool fabric, each 60 x 10 inches
2 pieces blue lining fabric, each 60 x 10 inches
1 2/3 yards medium-weight interfacing, 18 inches wide

24

1/2 yard yellow broadcloth or wool, 45 inches wide
scraps of medium blue, light blue, gold, navy blue
   fabrics
1/2 yard of fusible webbing, 18 inches wide
blue, yellow thread
yellow, orange six-strand embroidery floss

Directions

Preparation. Prepare the shaped stole pattern
(page 9). Trace the star of David pattern on
paper (page 26).

Make the patterns for the letters *J*, *e*, *s*, and *u*
(page 9). Enlarge the capital *J* to five inches
high and the lower case *e*, *s*, and *u* to three inches
high.

Cutting. Cut the stole from the wool fabric using
the shaped stole pattern.

Cut two medium blue pieces of fabric seven
inches square.

Cut the letters and the star of David out of
yellow fabric, each with fusible webbing.

Construction. Fuse the two *J*'s, each on one of
the medium blue squares. Machine appliqué the
raw edges with yellow thread.

Baste the blue squares to the stole fronts, 28
inches from the bottom of the stole. Finish the
edges of the blue squares with blue satin stitching.

Fuse the rest of the letters onto the stole fronts.
Machine appliqué the raw edges with yellow
thread.

Add bands of various colors (light blue, gold,
navy blue) across the stole above and below the
lettered sections. Cutting a variety of widths, pin
or baste them in place and finish the raw edges
with a satin stitch. Try a little designing of your
own, changing the colors or the widths until you
are satisfied with the basic design. When all the
stitching is complete, press the appliqués on the
back sides.

Seam the center back and press the seam open.
Fuse a yellow star of David across the center back
of the stole. Machine appliqué the raw edges in
yellow thread.

Machine couch three rows of six-strand embroidery floss between the horizontal decorative bands
and around the back neck as shown in the illustration. Interface and line the stole.

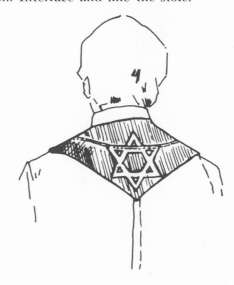

FLEUR-DE-LIS STOLE

A favorite emblem of kings, the fleur-de-lis can be used to suggest the King of kings. Fleurs-de-lis can be appliquéd to several different fabrics which are then assembled into the long strips of a stole. Experiment with this Advent stole by stitching a variety of fabrics, some dark-colored, some medium-toned, some light. On each section appliqué a fleur-de-lis in contrasting blue tones.

Materials

1/4 yard each grey satin, grey corduroy, pale blue corduroy, medium blue corduroy, 45 inches wide
1/2 yard teal blue velveteen, 45 inches wide
1/2 yard fusible webbing, 18 inches wide
1 2/3 yards medium-weight interfacing, 18 inches wide
1 piece lining fabric, 60 x 20 inches
blue, grey thread
dark blue six-strand embroidery floss

Directions

Preparation. Trace the fleur-de-lis pattern on paper.

Make a pattern for the upper stole fronts by measuring 36 inches from the bottom of the stole pattern (page 9). From that point to the back neck seam becomes the upper stole front pattern.

Cutting. Cut two pieces of pale blue corduroy (each 7 1/2 x 8 1/2 inches), two pieces of pale grey corduroy (each 7 1/2 x 8 1/2 inches), and two pieces of teal blue velveteen (each 7 1/2 x 20 inches). These pieces form the lower stole sections.

Using the fleur-de-lis pattern, cut six grey satin fleurs-de-lis and two medium blue corduroy fleurs-de-lis, each with fusible webbing.

Cut two pieces measuring 7 1/2 x 3 inches out of the grey corduroy.

Using the upper stole pattern you made, cut the upper stole sections out of the teal blue velveteen.

Construction. Fuse a grey satin fleur-de-lis on each of the pale blue pieces (centered), at the top of each of the teal blue pieces, and at the bottom of each of the upper stole pieces (see the illustration). Machine appliqué with grey thread. Fuse a medium blue fleur-de-lis on each of the grey pieces (centered). Machine appliqué with blue thread.

Sew the pieces together into two strips to form the lower stole sections: teal blue at the bottom, grey next, then pale blue. At the top of each strip

sew the 7 1/2 x 3 inch grey piece. Use a 1/2 inch seam allowance. Decorate the grey piece with couched lines of embroidery floss.

Sew the upper stole sections to the lower stole sections. Press all seams and appliqués on the back. Stitch the stole fronts together at the back neck seam. Press the seam open. Interface and line the stole.

BANDED STOLE

"Blessed is the King who comes in the name of the Lord! Peace in heaven and glory in the highest!" *(Luke 19:38).*

Set the mood for Advent using color alone, and at the same time make use of the special pieces of fabric saved from your past sewing projects. Blues and yellows combine well to express the joy of Advent; yellows and golds, colors of sun and light, contrast with blue to give it zest and life. Add more blues—some darker, some lighter—to make the other colors even more vivid.

Materials

If you select fabrics in the fall for the coming Advent season, you will find a good variety of corduroys, velveteens, and wools. Check through the blues for subtle and deep hues. Purchase 1 2/3 yards each of basic stole fabric, lining fabric, and interfacing. Then select swatches of blues and yellows from your fabric remnants at home to decorate the blue stole.

Directions

Preparation. Prepare one of the stole patterns (page 9).

Cutting. Using the stole pattern, cut out the basic stole from the fabric you purchased.

Construction. Experiment with a variety of color bands, cut from your remnants. Pin them in place on the basic stole, then stand back for a look to make sure you arrive at the best possible design.

Machine appliqué the bands in place and add decorative touches of your own. Sew the stole fronts together at the back neck seam. Press the seam open. Finish the stole with interfacing and lining.

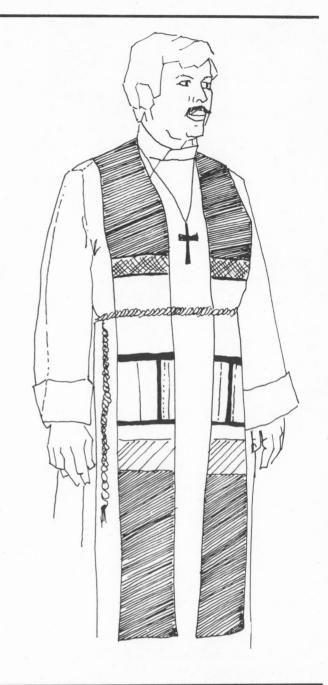

ADVENT FAIR

An Advent fair is an excellent kick-off festival for the Advent season. It is an idea center for families who like to prepare for Christmas at home during Advent. Participants at the fair offer their creative talents in cooking, crafts, or folklore to those who attend, giving them hints, recipes, and information for doing the activities themselves at home.

This is your chance to bring out the colors, fabrics, and symbols of Advent to display them for a closer look, especially for children. Include the pastor's vestments and worship paraments in the display. You can be available to answer questions about Advent symbols and to offer the fabrics for others to touch and enjoy.

Any of the designs for Advent altar cloths, pulpit or lectern cloths, stoles, or chasubles given in this chapter can be adapted to make marvelous Advent banners. Here are more design ideas for Advent banners. By using the basic techniques outlined in Chapter 3, you can create these banners.

LAMP AND HEART BANNER

You could use the lamp and heart symbol in repetition, applying it to many small banners to indicate preparation for the coming King. Hung in rows, the design creates an avenue, a way. Proceed down the "way," expressing the joy with which we receive the Savior. Or, you might arrange the lamp and heart symbols in rows on a single large banner.

See page 45 for the lamp symbol.

SCRIPTURE BANNERS

You could highlight the themes of Advent by picturing scriptural images on four banners, one for each week in Advent. Begin with the signs of the second coming of Christ. Luke 21:25-26 tells of the signs in the sun, moon and stars, the roaring of the sea, the distress and fear of the nations. Create this mood of the fear of the Lord with rough burlap background fabric for the first banner on the First Sunday in Advent. Use strident, shocking colors and diagonal slashing lines on the design layout to disturb the viewer.

Then, on the Second Sunday in Advent, add a banner with a penitent mood. Luke 21:25-36 suggests the use of the fig tree image; Luke 3:7-18 tells of the axe laid to the root of trees that bear no fruit.

For the Third Sunday in Advent, a banner with a mood of hope can be created by stressing horizontal lines in the design, subtle, rich, cool colors, pale silver stars, lights, or flowers.

A final, brighter banner with a heightened mood of anticipation can be made with hot colors on deep navy or violet-blue backgrounds for the Fourth Sunday in Advent. Create order and excitement with repeated symbols leading toward a focal point.

HYMN BANNERS

Use hymns to inspire bannermaking. Select hymns that supply visual images, particularly those that speak of light. Many Advent hymns will give you ideas to illustrate, but these present powerful images:

"O Lord, how shall I meet you"
"Come, O precious Ransom, come"
"Rejoice, rejoice, believers"
"Prepare the royal highway"
"Wake, awake, for night is flying"
"Fling wide the door, unbar the gate"
"Oh, come, oh, come Emmanuel"

UNDECORATED ALTAR CLOTHS

Fabrics, without any kind of symbol or design, can suggest a different mood for each Sunday in Advent. Try a rough blue burlap altar cloth for the First Sunday in Advent, with its theme of "the fear of the Lord." Change the cloth to purple burlap to suggest the penitent heart on the Second Sunday in Advent. On the Third and Fourth Sundays in Advent, build a mood of hope and anticipation for the coming of the King by using purple or blue velveteen or velvet on the altar.

The Christmas Season

Great excitement bursts forth on Christmas Day. We are once again amazed at the newborn child lying in a manger. Just as Mary wrapped her innocent babe in swaddling clothes, we cover the altar with our best white cloths.

If we were to weave church fabrics from natural fibers without the benefit of bleach and modern cleaning fluids, we would discover, as ancient weavers did, that a clean, white fabric is hard to make. The fibers of wool, cashmere, silk, and linen spin into an array of buffs, tans, browns, greys, and off-whites, but a pure white fiber is rare in nature. Weavers set aside their finest spinnings for church fabrics, those that were without imperfections, were clean, free from spot or stain, and light in color. The whitest cloths, the most difficult to achieve and to keep clean, were reserved for the highest worship celebrations.

Today we still cherish the white fabrics, and with our use of them we suggest the nature of Christ: untouched, pure, fair, free from spot or stain. The following pages suggest the making of paraments, vestments, and banners from white fabrics for the celebrations surrounding the Christmas season.

SUN OF RIGHTEOUSNESS ALTAR CLOTH

"The people who walked in darkness have seen a great light; those who dwelt in a land of deep darkness, on them has light shined" (Isaiah 9:2).

The phrase, "sun of righteousness" from Malachi 4:2 brings a striking symbol to the celebration of The Nativity of Our Lord. After the blues of Advent, the gleaming white and gold satin fabrics interchanged with the matte finish of brushed corduroy glow under the lights of Christmas.

The cloth illustrated here hangs on an altar 37 inches high, but you can adapt the design to fit your altar. The sun hanging does require more than a beginner's skill to complete. Besides fabric appliqué techniques, the project requires quiltmaker's skills for embellishing the appliqué work. The quilting strengthens the large hanging, keeping it firmly in shape, and the quilted surface invites a play of light on the shining symbol.

Size

The finished size for the hanging is 37 x 27 inches and does not include the depth.

Materials

3/4 yard off-white brushed corduroy, 45 inches wide
1/2 yard gold satin, 45 inches wide
3/4 yard white flannel-backed satin, 45 inches wide
1/4 yard gold and brown printed crepe satin
1/2 yard fusible webbing
3 yards gold satin piping
1 piece quilt batting, 37 x 27 inches
3/4 yard gold lining fabric for back (optional)
gold, white thread

Directions

Preparation. Enlarge the pattern as specified. Because many of the shapes are similar to each other, number the pattern pieces.

Cutting. Cut the off-white corduroy to a piece measuring 39 x 31 inches.

Cut out the other pieces of the design, following the diagram and the color key. The unlettered areas indicate the white corduroy background. The dotted lines indicate gold zigzag stitching lines on

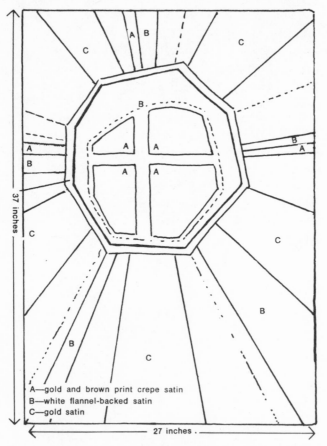

A—gold and brown print crepe satin
B—white flannel-backed satin
C—gold satin

the white corduroy. Cut fusible webbing pieces with all pieces of the sun design and the other pieces labeled A and B.

Construction. Begin the appliqué by making the central shape of the sun from colors A and B: Fuse the four A shapes cut from printed crepe satin to the white satin sun shape to form the cross. Machine appliqué around the A shapes with gold thread before basting the white sun to its place on the white corduroy backing.

The gold C shape around the white sun shape will be the final shape you will fuse to the appliqué; it covers the ends of the stitching lines of the sun's rays.

Next, fuse the three narrow A sun rays to the corduroy background. Repeat for the B sun rays cut from white satin. Machine appliqué the rays with matching thread.

Then, hand baste the C shapes to the corduroy background. The sizes of these rays are too large for fusing. Machine appliqué with gold thread.

Finally, fuse the sun C shape you set aside earlier around the white B sun shape. A careful fit is important. Appliqué with gold thread.

Embellish the cloth by stitching wide gold zigzagged lines along the dotted lines indicated in the pattern. Then, using a dressmaker's cutting board as a guide, trim the edges to make it straight, with neat 90° angle corners. Trim the sides and bottom edges of the hanging with gold satin piping. Press raw edges toward the back to reveal the gold piped edges.

Finally, lay the hanging over a 37 x 27 inch piece of quilt batting, pin the two layers together and quilt along the edges of the appliquéd pieces with a running stitch. Also, quilt around sides and bottom edges 1/2 inch from the gold piping.

Complete the altar cloth with the depth to fit your altar. The altar cloth can be lined with a gold satin fabric, but the lining may pull the hanging out of shape. Sometimes large pieces such as this are better left unlined.

SUN OF RIGHTEOUSNESS CHASUBLE

A chasuble featuring the Sun of Righteousness design might be a worthy companion to the Sun of Righteousness altar cloth. The main body of the chasuble is sewn together with seams (1/2-inch seam allowance), not appliquéd. The sun design is appliquéd onto that main body piece. The sun design might be appliquéd to the front only, the back only, or both front and back. The quilted layer is eliminated; the chasuble is lined instead.

Materials

First, prepare the pattern pieces (see *Preparation* below). Determine which fabric will be used for each piece. Although the divisions are not exactly as the altar cloth, you may want to follow a similar color arrangement. Then, lay the pieces for each color out as a separate 45-inch wide area. This will show the lengths of fabric needed.

Directions

Preparation. Enlarge the pattern as specified. Make two patterns, one for the master pattern and one for cutting out the design. Number and color code each piece on both patterns.

Cutting. Cut each piece out of the selected fabric. Because the pieces which make up the main body

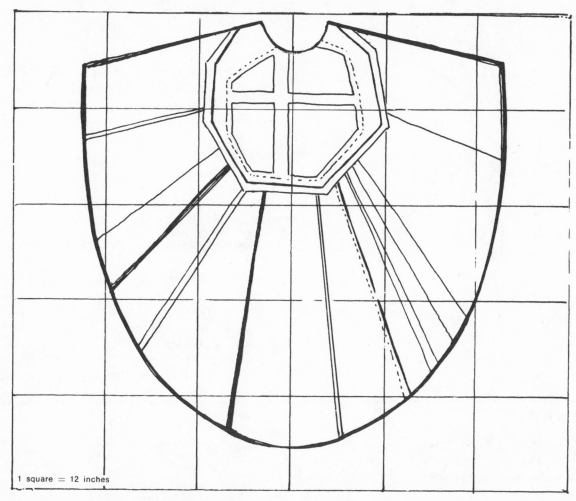

1 square = 12 inches

of the chasuble are to be pieced together with seams, add 1/2-inch seam allowance to all pattern pieces. The sun design, since it will be appliquéd, requires no seam allowance. Cut fusible webbing with the sun design.

Construction. Sew the pieces which make up the front of the chasuble together, using a 1/2-inch seam allowance. Do the same for the back of the chasuble. Press all seams open.

Fuse and appliqué the sun design onto the front and/or back of the chasuble, following the directions for the Sun of Righteousness altar cloth (page 31). Press the appliqué on the back side.

Sew the side seams of the chasuble together and press. Line the chasuble.

STAR PULPIT/LECTERN CLOTH

This companion piece for the pulpit or lectern features the star of Bethlehem. Effective lighting will catch the sheen of the white satin appliqué. Not only useful for the Sundays in Christmas, this cloth also offers a powerful light theme for The Epiphany of Our Lord.

Size

The finished size for the illustrated parament is 32 x 14 inches and includes both drop and depth to fit most pulpit or lectern bookrests. Check these dimensions with your chancel furnishings.

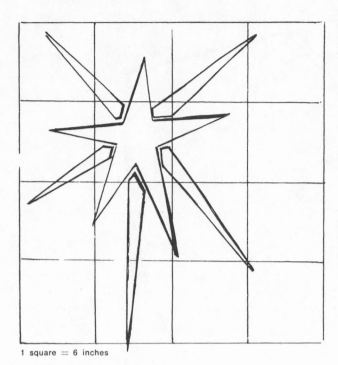

1 square = 6 inches

Materials

1 piece dark gold upholstery velveteen, 36 x 16 inches

1/4 yard white satin, 45 inches wide

1 piece medium-weight interfacing, 32 x 14 inches

1 piece gold lining fabric, 36 x 16 inches

white, gold thread

Directions

Preparation. Enlarge the star pattern as specified.

Cutting. Using the pattern, cut the star from white satin with fusible webbing.

Construction. Fuse the star to the background fabric, positioning it according to the illustration. Machine appliqué the raw edges with white thread.

Roll over edges of the cloth one inch along the edges and press toward the back side. Interface and line the cloth.

Finish the cloth with a channel or whatever is necessary for the particular pulpit or lectern.

STAR STOLE

A stole studded with stars sparkles at the celebration of The Nativity of Our Lord. It, too, supplements the motifs surrounding the great light, the Sun of Righteousness.

The materials will yield two stoles.

Materials

1 2/3 yards white corduroy or wool blend fabric, 45 inches wide

1 2/3 yards lining fabric, 45 inches wide

1 2/3 yards medium-weight interfacing, 18 inches wide

1/2 yard gold satin

1/2 yard fusible webbing

white, gold thread

Directions

Preparation. Prepare a stole pattern (page 9). Enlarge the star (page 18) to twice its size.

Cutting. Using the stole pattern, cut the stole pieces out of the white fabric.

Cut eight stars for each stole from gold satin and fusible webbing.

Construction. Position the stars on the background material, four on each side of the stole fronts. Place some of the stars along the edges, so they

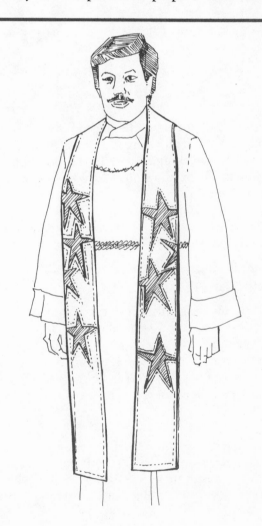

show only partially. This placement gives a feeling that there are more stars, that the star design continues on. When showing the stars partially, place at least 2/3 of the star shape on the stole front. If less of the star shape is seen, it will appear only as a point or intrusion on the total design.

ORNAMENTS FOR THE CHRISTMAS TREE

The majestic evergreen tree, a favorite Christmas symbol, refreshes this season with its message of hope. The lives of Christians are ever green, filled with the daily freshness of life because of the coming of Jesus Christ.

Ornament your church's tree this year with appliqué. The blending of soft fabrics with the prickly needles makes a lively contrast of textures. Add lighting and garlanding to complete the decorations.

Materials
fusible webbing
fabric glue
white and gold fabrics
white felt
brown felt
quilt batting
white, gold thread

Directions
Preparation. To make the patterns, trace the symbol shapes (page 36) on paper. You might also want to use other symbols pictured in this book (for example, fleur-de-lis, star). Enlarge these symbol shapes to a comparable size.

Cutting. Using the patterns, cut the symbol shapes from white fabric and fusible webbing. Cut six-inch square pieces from gold fabric—as many pieces as there are symbols.

Construction. Fuse the white symbol to the center of the gold square. Machine appliqué the symbols' edges with white thread. Steam press the back of the appliqué.

Pin a layer of quilt batting behind the ornament. Leaving a 3/4-inch border all around the white symbol, trim away any excess gold fabric and quilt batting. Pin the padded shape to white felt and baste the three layers together around the raw edges. Machine appliqué over the basting line with gold thread.

Install a gold eyelet in the white felt at the top of the ornament for a hanger.

Fuse the stars in place. Machine appliqué the raw edges with gold thread. Press the appliqué on the back.

Finally, sew the stole fronts together at the back neck seam. Press the seam open. Interface and line the stole.

Leaving a 1/4-inch border of the white felt around the padded symbol, trim away any excess felt.

With fabric glue, attach dark brown felt to the manger ornament to represent hay, and a "jewel" to the crown.

GARLAND CHASUBLE

"For as the earth brings forth its shoots, and as a garden causes what is sown in it to spring up, so the Lord God will cause righteousness and praise to spring forth before all the nations" (Isaiah 61:11).

Directions

Preparation. Prepare the long chasuble pattern (page 8). Trace the daisy and leaf patterns on paper.

Cutting. Taking advantage of the 60-inch width

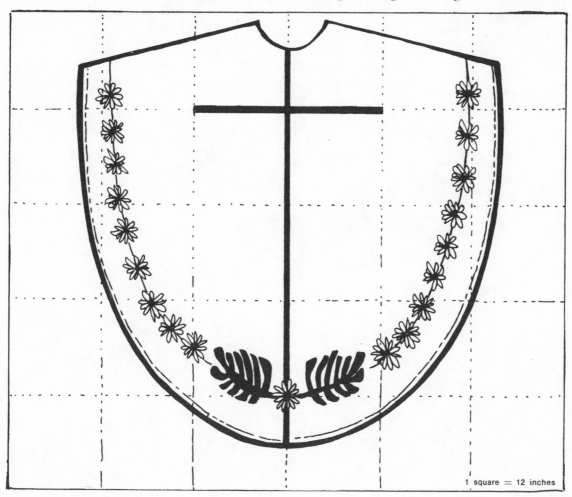

1 square = 12 inches

Bedeck a white chasuble with gold flowers and greenery to illustrate this Christmas text. This is an excellent time to introduce the chasuble vestment to your congregation if your pastor has not yet worn one. The chasuble can highlight the communion service.

Materials

3 1/2 yards sturdily woven white drapery fabric, 60 inches wide
1/2 yard bright gold cotton
1/4 yard dark green cotton
1 yard fusible webbing
10 yards dark green single fold braid trim
2 yards green flat braid, 1 inch wide
1 skein dark green embroidery floss

of the drapery fabric, cut the back and front of the long chasuble without center seams.

If you wish to decorate only the front or the back of the chasuble, cut 19 daisies from the gold fabric and two leaves from the green fabric, each with fusible webbing. If you will decorate front and back, cut 38 daisies and four leaves.

Construction. Position the daisies and leaves according to the illustration and fuse them in place. Machine appliqué them using matching thread.

Handstitch flat braid at the center front and/or back to form the cross.

Sew the front and back together at the side seams. Press the seams open. Trim hem and neck edges with folded braid trim.

Embellish the garland by embroidering vines between the flowers.

GARLAND STOLE

The stole graphically states that Jesus causes the earth to bring forth its shoots and a garden to spring up.

Materials

1 yard white woven fabric, 45 inches wide
1/2 yard pale green trigger cloth
scraps of bright gold and off-white fabrics
1/4 yard fusible webbing
1 2/3 yards medium-weight interfacing, 18 inches wide
1 2/3 yards lining fabric, 18 inches wide
dark green embroidery floss
white, gold, green thread

Directions

Preparation. Prepare patterns of the capital letters *I, H,* and *S.* The letters should be five inches high.

Trace the daisy pattern from the Garland Chasuble design. See page 78 for leaf pattern.

Make a pattern for the upper stole fronts by measuring 36 inches from the bottom of the full-size stole pattern (page 9). From that point to the back neck seam becomes the upper stole front pattern.

Cutting. Cut two daisies from white fabric and two five-inch circles from gold fabric, each with fusible webbing.

Cut two strips, 18 x 8 inches each, from the green fabric. Cut two strips, 20 x 8 inches each, from white fabric.

Using the pattern you prepared, cut the upper stole sections from white fabric.

Cut two each of the letters, *I, H, S,* from white fabric, each with fusible webbing. Cut 12 leaves from green fabric, each with fusible webbing.

Construction. Position a daisy in the center of each circle, fuse, and machine appliqué with white thread.

Position the gold circles on the upper stole fronts, centered, three inches from the bottom. Fuse, and machine appliqué with gold thread. Position two green leaves below each circle (see illustration), fuse, and machine appliqué, using green thread.

Position four green leaves on each of the white strips (see illustration). Fuse, and machine appliqué with green thread.

Center the letters *I H S* on each of the green strips to form the Christ monogram. Fuse, and machine appliqué with white thread.

Seam the appliquéd upper stole fronts to the appliquéd green strips. Then seam that to the white strips to complete the stole. Press all seams open and all appliqués on the back side.

Embellish the flowers with couched lines of embroidery floss for stems.

Sew the stole fronts together at the back neck seam. Press the seam open.

Interface and line the stole.

CROSS AND CROWN STOLE

Cut out the crosses and crowns from the tree ornament project and apply them to an off-white stole for the Sundays of the Christmas season. Appliqué a cross or crown to the center of eight eight-inch squares of various off-white fabrics, and you have the two lower halves of the stole fronts!

Materials

8 pieces of various off-white homespun fabrics, 8 x 8 inches
1 yard canvas fabric, 18 inches wide
1/4 yard white kettlecloth
1/4 yard fusible webbing, 18 inches wide
1 skein dark grey embroidery floss
1 2/3 yards medium-weight interfacing fabric, 18 inches wide
1 2/3 yards lining fabric, 18 inches wide
grey thread

Directions

Preparation. Trace the cross, crown, and anchor symbol patterns (page 36) on paper.

Make a pattern for the upper stole fronts by measuring 29 inches from the bottom of the full-size stole pattern (page 9). From that point to the back neck seam becomes the upper stole front pattern.

Cutting. Using the symbol patterns, cut the symbol shapes from white kettlecloth—cut two anchors, four crosses, and four crowns, each with fusible webbing.

Cut the upper parts of the stole from the canvas fabrics using the pattern you prepared.

Construction. Center the white symbols on the off-white squares, and fuse them in place. Machine appliqué the raw edges of the symbols with dark grey thread (to give the shapes a distinctive outline).

Add another outline by couching six-strand embroidery floss 1/2 inch from the grey appliqué stitching.

Seam four of the appliquéd squares together to form one side of the stole (top to bottom: cross, anchor, crown, cross). Repeat for the other side.

Center the remaining crowns at the bottom ends of the upper stole fronts (see illustration). Fuse them in place; machine appliqué and couch embroidery floss as on the squares.

Seam the lower stole fronts to the upper stole fronts. Press seams open and press appliqués on the back. Add couched lines of grey embroidery floss along both sides of each seam as shown in the illustration.

To complete the stole, seam the center back and press the seam open. Interface and line the stole.

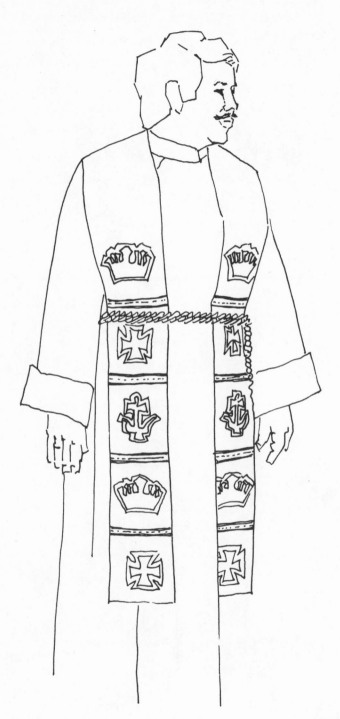

The Epiphany Season

The Christmas Cycle closes with the Epiphany Season and its joyous celebration of light. The season moves from the star of Bethlehem, to the river Jordan where Jesus performed his first miracle, to the synagogues where Jesus taught. The season culminates in the transfiguration of the Sun of Righteousness.

The season opens with a festival—The Baptism of Our Lord (First Sunday after the Epiphany)—and closes with a festival—The Transfiguration of Our Lord (Last Sunday after the Epiphany). For both these festivals the color is white. During the time between these festivals we celebrate vigorous spiritual growth brought by Christ's teachings and his presence here on earth. The color for the season is green, the color of new beginnings, new life, new energy, new hope. It is a time to learn, to develop, to rejoice. Green, the natural color for a season of growth, suggests the earthly aspects of God in our lives, and of Christ's public ministry. Scripture texts for the Season after the Epiphany picture Christ as the Good Shepherd who leads his sheep to green pastures, feeds the flocks with his teachings, and restores lost ones to the fold.

The tradition for using green during neutral seasons or on the Sundays that fall between the special festivals of Jesus Christ probably developed for practical reasons. If we were to dye fabrics for church use as weavers of old did, we would discover that the earth provides a wealth of plants and vegetables for green, brown, yellow, orange, and grey dyes. They are everywhere. The common dandelion, dock, goldenrod, mullein, mustard, pokeweed, Queen Anne's lace, marigold, and daylilies provide a great variety of yellow, green, and brown dyes. Carrots, onions, beets, spinach, berries, fruits of the vine, and tree twigs offer still more of the earth-colored hues.

Handling color for the Season after the Epiphany may be more difficult than the other seasons because greens and browns tend to be more neutral than scarlets, blues, or purples. Combinations of colors can become indistinct, so similar in lightness or darkness that shapes are unclear from a distance. When selecting fabrics, choose contrasting colors so that the appliqué can be read.

THE EPIPHANY OF OUR LORD CHASUBLE

"Now when Jesus was born in Bethlehem of Judea in the days of Herod the king, behold, wise men from the East came to Jerusalem, saying, 'Where is he who has been born king of the Jews? For we have seen his star in the East, and have come to worship him'" (Matthew 2:1-2).

To create the mood for this festive occasion, you might use the Sun of Righteousness altar cloth and Star cloth from the Christmas season. Highlight the day with a chasuble displaying a border of small stars surrounding a large star.

Design this garment yourself: Set white stars on gold background fabrics, the center panel a lighter or darker shade than the outside panels. Or, cut the large center star from gold and appliqué it on a white background; then, reverse the colors on the outside sections of the chasuble—white stars on a gold background.

For fabrics, you might use brushed corduroys, velveteens, satins, or wools. Because gold and white are both light colors, the shapes may be unclear from a distance so you might use brown outlines around the stars. You might also embellish the lines of the chasuble with drapery cording or braided trim.

THE BAPTISM OF OUR LORD CLOTHS

"Behold my servant, whom I uphold, my chosen, in whom my soul delights; I have put my Spirit upon him" (Isaiah 42:1).

A single design can be used in many ways to prepare for the festival of Christ's baptism. For the chasuble appliqué, for example, the design is enlarged to 55 inches high. Or, the same appliqué might be enlarged to only 24 inches high and positioned, one on each of the shoulders of the chasuble.

You can be the designer. Adapt the flame and dove for use in your sanctuary. First, decide on the cloths you would like to make—chasuble, stole, lectern/pulpit cloth, or altar cloth—and determine their finished sizes. Then, cut newsprint paper to fit those sizes. Tack the papers cut to size on the wall and project the dove and/or flame image onto the newsprint. Pull the projector back and forth until you come to a composition that pleases you. Some people prefer large, graphic designs that exceed the boundaries of the cloth, while others like a small symbol set in a lower corner or central position. The possibilities are endless.

A—light grey
B—orange-gold
C—orange
D—orange-red
E—red-orange
F—red

Draw your final design onto the paper mock-ups with a black marking pen. This will be your master pattern. Make a copy of this master for a pattern to use when cutting out the pieces for the fabric appliqué.

Select fabric for the cloths and the appliqués. The cloths should be white—the color of The Baptism of Our Lord—but you could apply red-oranges, oranges, and yellow-oranges to the white fabrics for the flames. Choice of fabrics is very important for this design. A light grey dove would be seen from a distance on the white cloth, but a white dove on the white cloth might be ineffective. The color key accompanying the diagram is only a suggestion, but it may get you started.

Step-by-step instructions for these projects are not included, since you are the designer, but you can refer to the Advent and Christmas projects for ideas on amounts of materials to purchase, as well as how to construct each piece.

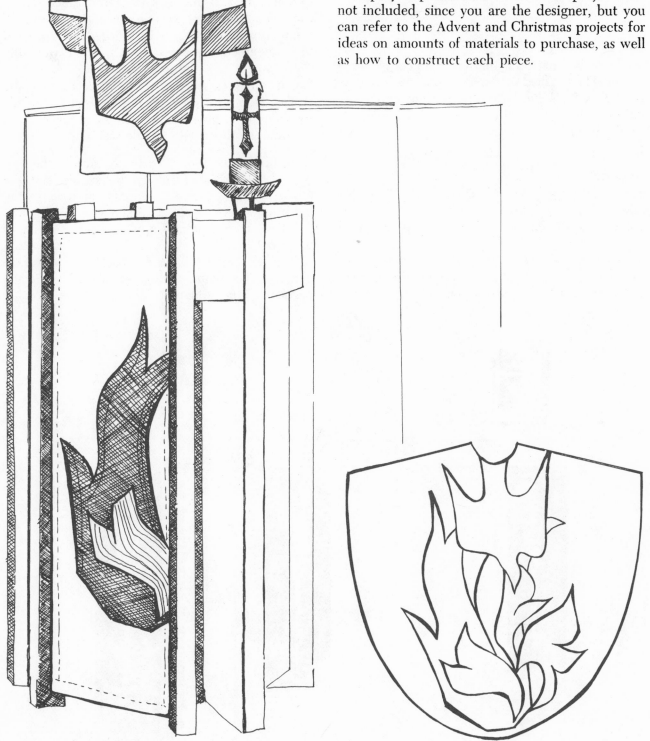

TORCH ALTAR AND FONT CLOTHS

Spread a spring green or pale green cloth on the altar. Light up the table with appliquéd torches, reminding the congregation that the spirit of the Lord is present. Repeat the motif on the baptismal font. Setting the fiery torches on dark green fabric strips contrasts with the lighter-toned altar cloth underneath.

Size

The finished size for the font hanging is 39 x 9 inches. The finished sizes for the altar hangings are each 37 x 10 inches. These measurements include only the drop. You will need to add the depth to fit the particular font or altar.

Materials

1 1/4 yards forest green woven fabric, 45 inches wide

1 1/4 yards medium-weight interfacing, 36 inches wide

1 1/4 yards dark green lining fabric, 45 inches wide

1/2 yard medium-toned grey-green trigger cloth

1/4 yard medium-bright red-orange trigger cloth

1/2 yard fusible webbing

orange, grey, dark green thread

Directions

Preparation. Enlarge the torch patterns to twice their size.

Cutting. Cut two pieces of the forest green fabric, each 39 x 12 inches; cut one piece 41 x 11 inches.

Cut three strips, each 10 x 1 1/4 inches, from the grey-green fabric, each with fusible webbing. These strips form the torch handles.

Cut three each of the torch pieces and the crosses from the grey-green fabric, with fusible webbing. Cut three each of the flame pieces from the orange fabric, with fusible webbing.

Construction. Position the torch pieces, the fire pieces, the strips for the torch handles, and the crosses according to the illustration. Reverse the torch motif on one of the altar pieces. Fuse them in place, then machine appliqué the raw edges with matching threads.

Press the appliqués on the back side. Interface and line the cloths, adding the depth to fit the particular altar and font.

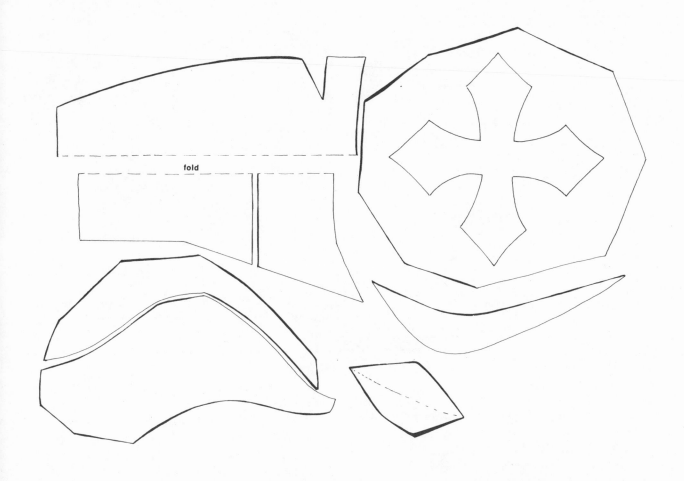

fold

LAMP PULPIT/LECTERN CLOTH

Size

The finished size for the Lamp cloth is 14 x 32 inches. This measurement includes both the drop and depth to fit an average-sized bookrest. Check these dimensions with the furnishings in your chancel.

Materials

1 piece dark green fabric, 16 x 34 inches
*1 yard interfacing, 28 inches wide
*1 yard green lining fabric, 45 inches wide
*1/2 yard medium-toned grey-green trigger cloth
*1/4 yard medium-bright red-orange trigger cloth
*1/8 yard black cotton
*1/2 yard fusible webbing, 18 inches wide
skein black embroidery floss
*black, orange, grey, green thread

---

* If both the Lamp and the Chi-Rho pulpit/lectern cloths are made, it is not necessary to duplicate these materials. For example, only one yard of green lining fabric provides enough material for both cloths.

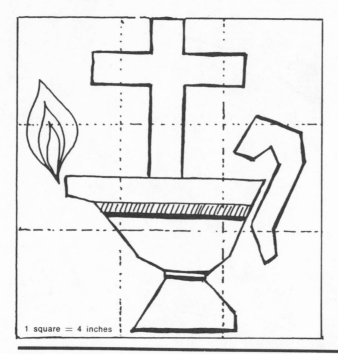

1 square = 4 inches

Directions

Preparation. Enlarge the lamp pattern as specified.

Cutting. Cut the pattern pieces from the fabric: lamp pieces from grey-green, flame pieces from red-orange, strip below lamp and flame outline from black, each with fusible webbing.

Construction. Position the appliqué pieces on the background fabric, according to the illustration, about four inches from the bottom edge.

Fuse the pieces in place, then machine appliqué raw edges with matching threads.

Embellish the lamp by machine couching embroidery floss across the lamp body and the base. Also, machine couch the embroidery floss 1/2 inch above the black strip.

Press the appliqué on the back side. Interface and line the cloth to fit the particular pulpit or lectern.

CHI-RHO PULPIT/LECTERN CLOTH

Size

The finished size for the Chi-Rho cloth is 14 x 32 inches. This measurement includes both the drop and the depth to fit an average-sized bookrest. Check these dimensions with the furnishings in your chancel.

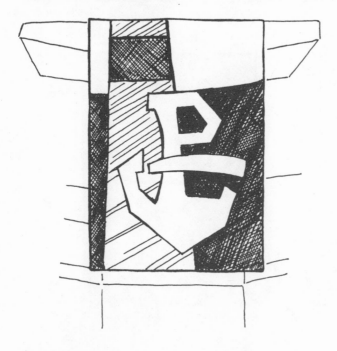

* If both the Lamp and the Chi-Rho pulpit/lectern cloths are made, it is not necessary to duplicate these materials. For example, only one yard of green lining fabric provides enough material for both cloths.

Materials

1 piece light green trigger cloth, 16 x 34 inches
° 1 yard interfacing, 28 inches wide
° 1 yard green lining fabric, 45 inches wide
° 1/2 yard medium-toned grey-green trigger cloth
° 1/4 yard medium-bright red-orange trigger cloth
° 1/8 yard black cotton
1/2 yard dark green trigger cloth
° 1/2 yard fusible webbing, 18 inches wide
black, orange, grey, green thread

Directions

Preparation. Enlarge the Chi-Rho pattern pieces as specified.

Cutting. Cut the Chi-Rho from the red-orange fabric, with fusible webbing.

Cut the vertical tapered strip from the grey-green fabric. This strip is the length of the drop; its width tapers from 4 1/2 inches at the top to 7 1/2 inches at the bottom.

Cut a piece of dark green or black fabric which will run across the tapered strip above the Chi-Rho (see the illustration). This strip should be as wide as the tapered strip and 3 1/4 inches high.

Cut the dark green cloth to make a piece 16 inches wide. Slope the top so the length moves from 14 3/4 to 16 inches (see illustration).

Construction. Hand baste the half yard length of dark green fabric to the lower part of the background fabric. Machine appliqué with matching thread.

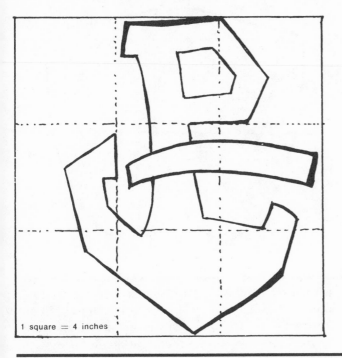

1 square = 4 inches

Baste the vertical tapered piece in place, and machine appliqué with matching thread. Baste the black strip over the tapered piece, and machine appliqué with black thread.

Position the Chi-Rho, fuse it in place, and machine appliqué with matching thread.

Press the appliqué on the back side. Interface and line the cloth to fit the particular pulpit or lectern.

THE TRANSFIGURATION OF OUR LORD CLOTHS

"And he was transfigured before them, and his face shone like the sun, and his garments became white as light" (Matthew 17:2).

For the celebration of The Transfiguration of Our Lord, create the "light" atmosphere by replacing the green paraments of the Sundays after the Epiphany with plain white cloths. Once again, use the basic white linen altar cloth. Add pulpit and lectern hangings of white linen or other woven cloth, banded perhaps, with white satin. The same banding could be applied to vestments for the day. Graphic symbols are not really necessary; the white color alone communicates the theme.

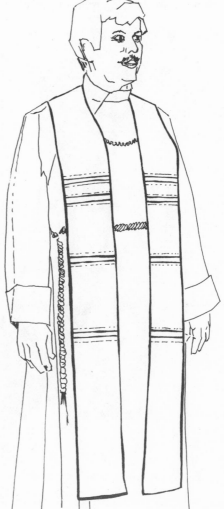

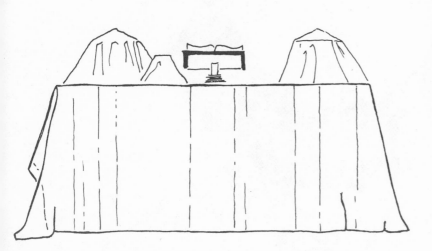

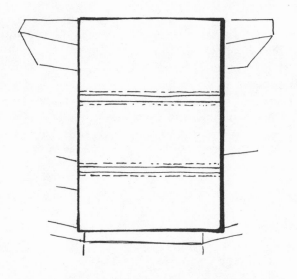 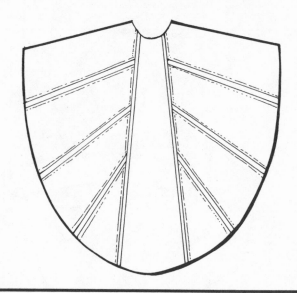

JEWELED BORDER CHASUBLE

"You shall be a crown of beauty in the hand of the Lord, and a royal diadem in the hand of your God" (Isaiah 62:3).

A medium-toned green chasuble bordered with jewel-toned fabric scraps of orange, gold, raw umber, and dark green describes Isaiah 62:3 in an abstract way. Choose a range of tones from light to dark to make the border sparkle. Trim it with small, sharp details at the edges of the patches and embroider dark crosses on patches of light colors.

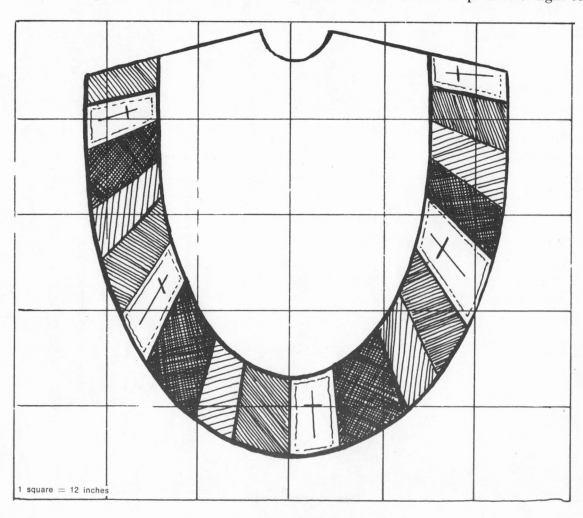

1 square = 12 inches

Chapter 5

THE EASTER CYCLE

The high mood of The Transfiguration of Our Lord suddenly changes to solemnity, and the color for Ash Wednesday is black. We realize our mortality. We die. We become dust.

The Easter Cycle, with its wide span of mood, provides an arts committee with exciting work. With color, fabric, symbol, and thread, you can share with your congregation the miracle of death and resurrection, the wonder of new life and rebirth. Your fabric appliqué work should reflect the same excitement as the Easter story itself.

The Easter Cycle begins with the preparatory season of Lent, rises to the high festival of The Resurrection of Our Lord, and continues the spirit of new life through the Easter season until it culminates with the Day of Pentecost.

The scriptural readings for the Sundays of the Easter cycle are filled with images of sin, then death, and finally new life. Ashes, sackcloth, the serpent, and the apple point to humanity's sinful nature and need for repentance. The cross, thorns, and blood tell of the sacrifice of Jesus Christ. The crowns, crosses, butterflies, and lilies tell of resurrection, victory over sin and death, and the rebirth of God's people through Jesus Christ.

The Lenten Season

The inward look of Lent begins on Ash Wednesday. The color of ash marks the soiled, stained, penitent soul. With the spreading of the ashes, the spring of the soul comes, when the soil is prepared and made ready for replanting.

Once the ashes have been spread and humility experienced, the Lenten season begins and the color indicative of the 40 days of preparation is purple. The receding character of purple makes a conducive atmosphere for reflection and repentance during worship.

Because of the difficulty in finding purple dyes, this color was traditionally reserved for royalty and limited church use. During Lent, we prepare for the King as we turn back for a look at the quality of our faith and life, reflecting on our Baptism into Christ's death.

When preparing the paraments and other visual elements for the season of Lent, you will want to develop a reflective theme. Begin, as you did for Advent, by removing extra decorative elements from the worship setting. Removing elements belonging to the Christmas Cycle is important. It will give you a new beginning.

For Lent, look to plain, dark purple or muslin-colored fabrics. A trace of red stitchery alluding to Christ's sacrifice and a limited use of symbols help create the reflective mood.

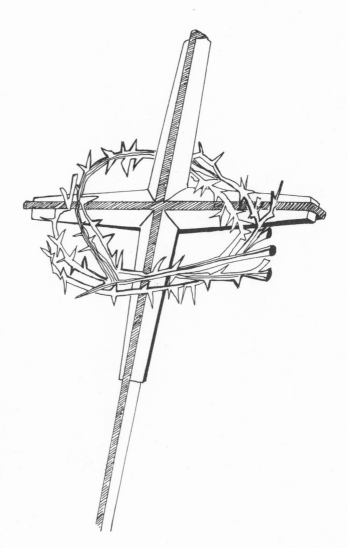

PENITENTIAL STOLE

"Have mercy on me, O God, according to thy steadfast love; according to thy abundant mercy blot out my transgressions. Wash me thoroughly from my iniquity, and cleanse me from my sin! . . . Purge me with hyssop, and I shall be clean; wash me, and I shall be whiter than snow" (Psalm 51:1-2, 7).

Mark the opening of the Lenten season with a Lenten vestment to symbolize your congregation's discipleship at the foot of the cross. Although the design seems abstract, the idea behind it is simple: The people of God move toward the foot of the cross for renewal. Beginning the pilgrimage with a large, dark band of black or dark grey at the hems of the stole, progress upward by appliquéing bands of deep purples, greys, mauves, and dark reds across the stole. The dark at the bottom symbolizes the ashes of Ash Wednesday; the purples, greys, and mauves represent the weeks of Lent; the scarlet laid over a band of unbleached linen cloth at the foot of the cross points to Holy Week. An unbleached linen cross appliquéd at the top of each progression on purple fabric finishes the design.

Take time to experiment with various color arrangements. Use your own design sense for determining the size of each piece.

See page 9 for stole patterns.

PENITENTIAL ALTAR CLOTH

To create an austere, low-key atmosphere for the season of Lent, stitch this simple four-panel altar cloth from plain fabrics. The instructions outline the construction of four cloths. The cloths hang in pairs, one a reflection of the other.

Size

The finished size for each piece is 16 x 33 inches. This includes only the drop. Additional cloth must be added for the depth.

Materials

2 yards deep purple fabric, 45 inches wide
1 yard unbleached linen, 36 inches wide
1 yard deep scarlet fabric, 45 inches wide
1 yard hot purple fabric, 12 inches wide
1 yard black fabric, 45 inches wide
7 yards interfacing, 18 inches wide
3 yards purple lining fabric, 45 inches wide
deep red, black, purple thread

Directions

Preparation. Enlarge the pattern pieces as specified.

Cutting. Cut four panels of purple fabric, each 18 x 35 inches.

Cut two unbleached linen pieces using pattern A, two using pattern B.

Cut the black and hot purple strips—two using pattern A and two using pattern B—adding 1/2 inch along the inside edges (which will be tucked under the linen piece).

Construction. Machine embroider a cross on each linen panel, using the pattern to indicate placement. To do machine embroidery, thread the machine with deep red thread and set the machine on a wide, close zigzag stitch. Press the back of the machine embroidery.

Position the hot purple, linen, and black pieces on the background cloth, two as pattern A and two as pattern B. The linen piece overlaps the hot purple and black pieces. Hand baste them in place.

Machine appliqué the linen strips first with tan thread, then machine appliqué the outer purple and black strips with purple and black thread. Press the appliqués on the back side, interface, and line them, adding the depth necessary for the particular altar.

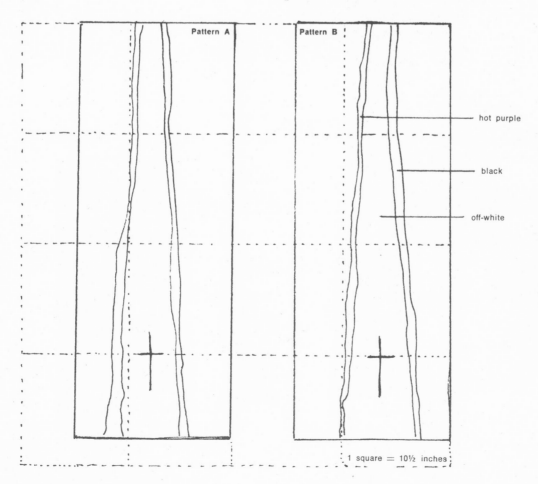

Pattern A   Pattern B

hot purple

black

off-white

1 square = 10½ inches

ASH WEDNESDAY AND HOLY WEEK OVERLAY CLOTHS

For Ash Wednesday and Holy Week, stitch overlays to accompany the Penitential Altar Cloth.

Sew four plain dark bands, 10 inches wide, to cover the four panels on Ash Wednesday.

Sew four scarlet bands, 10 inches wide, to cover the four panels during Holy Week. A possible design for these bands is pictured on page 54.

LENTEN LESSON PULPIT/LECTERN CLOTH

For each Sunday in Lent make a pulpit or lectern hanging which illustrates that day's theme. Make simple bands in Lenten purple to hang from the lectern or pulpit, adding simple appliqués which feature an object selected from five Old Testament lessons prescribed for Lent. You might also add machine or hand embroidery in the same style you applied to the altar cloth.

Here are five ideas which point out our sinfulness and God's plan for reconciliation. These cloths are designed to accompany some readings from lectionary series A and some from series B.

Patterns for the symbols can be copied from these illustrations, from Sunday school curriculum, from children's coloring books or storybooks, or drawn freehand.

The Star of Jacob Cloth (page 20) supplies dimensions and instructions for cutting and constructing this type of lectern/pulpit cloth.

First Sunday in Lent—Series A

"Now the serpent was more subtle than any other wild creature that the Lord God had made. He said to the woman, 'Did God say, "You shall not eat of any tree of the garden?"'" (Genesis 3:1).

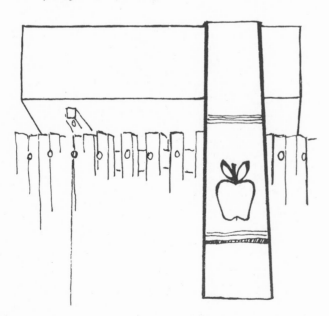

Second Sunday in Lent—Series A

"Then the Lord appeared to Abram, and said, 'To your descendants I will give this land.' So he built there an altar to the Lord" (Genesis 12:7).

Third Sunday in Lent—Series B

"And God spoke all these words, saying, 'I am the Lord your God, who brought you out of the land of Egypt, out of the house of bondage. You shall have no other gods before me'" (Exodus 20:1-3).

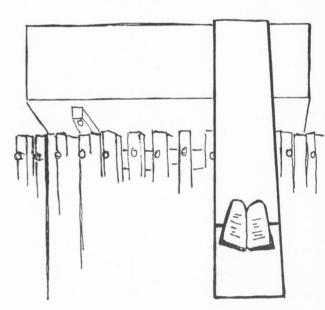

Fourth Sunday in Lent—Series B

"So Moses made a bronze serpent, and set it on a pole; and if a serpent bit any man, he would look at the bronze serpent and live" (Numbers 21:9).

Fifth Sunday in Lent—Series B

"I will put my law within them, and I will write it upon their hearts; and I will be their God and they shall be my people" (Jeremiah 31:33).

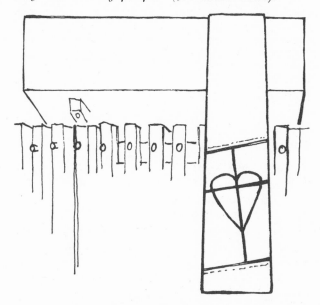

Holy Week

Scarlet or deep red, the color of passion, blood, and victory inspires the spirit of Holy Week. We remember Christ's passion, understanding that red is not ultimately an angry, death color, but the color of a victorious triumph over death. God claims us from death, freeing us to live with new passion and spirit.

SUNDAY OF THE PASSION BANNERS

These banners celebrate the triumph of the cross of Jerusalem. Carry them high on poles in the Procession with Palms on Sunday of the Passion. Adorned with victory banners, palm branches, and the red vestments of the day, this festival has potential for glory and beauty unique to any other celebration of the year. This is the day to hang the red overlays you made to lay atop the Lenten paraments.

Size

Determine the size and number of banners by looking at your worship space. Perhaps one large processional banner would have the most impact. Or, if your space has a vast, open wall at the front of the room, several banners might be appropriate.

Materials

Large pieces of deep red felt
White felt
Purple felt
Green felt
Fabric glue or matching thread

Directions

Preparation. Determine the size of your banner(s). Enlarge the pattern given to the appropriate size (see page 9).

Cutting. Cut the background red felt in the size and shape you have determined. Felt does not require finishing hems. However, do allow fabric for the channel through which the banner rod goes.

Using the pattern, cut the circle out of white felt, the Jerusalem cross and the ring out of purple felt, and the palm branches out of green felt.

Construction. Turn the top three to four inches of the banner fabric back and stitch it to create a channel for the banner rod.

Center the Jerusalem cross and the ring in the white circle and attach them, either by machine appliqué or gluing.

Position the white circle and the palm branches on the red background felt. Attach them, either by machine appliqué or gluing.

This may be a very good crafts project for Sunday school students. You can adapt the design

simply by making the measurements of the banner a manageable size for them. Then have the children cut the elements of the design from felt or paper. Older children often like the security of patterns while some younger ones see no need for them. Show the younger children your finished example, supply them with materials, and stand back! Watch them cut their own ideas of palm branches and crosses. You will be amazed at the freshness of their designs and the freedom with which they approach the project.

HOSANNA STOLE

"And those who went before and those who followed cried out, 'Hosanna! Blessed is he who comes in the name of the Lord! Blessed is the kingdom of our father David that is coming! Hosanna in the highest!' "(Mark 11:9-10).

Materials

2 pieces scarlet fabric, each 60 x 10 inches
2 pieces scarlet lining fabric, each 60 x 10 inches
1 2/3 yards medium weight interfacing, 18 inches
    wide
fabric for lettering (keep it low-key to relate to
    the solemnity of the service)
fusible webbing
scarlet thread

Directions

Preparation. Prepare the shaped stole pattern (page 9).

Make capital letter patterns for the word *Hosanna*. The letters should be as high as the finished stole is wide.

Cutting. Using the stole pattern, cut the stole from the scarlet fabric. Cut two sets of letters from the selected fabric, with fusible webbing.

Construction. Position the letters on the stole, following the illustration. Fuse them in place and machine appliqué.

Press the appliqué on the back side. Stitch the back neck seam of the stole. Interface and line the stole.

MAUNDY THURSDAY CLOTHS

"And as they were eating, he took bread, and blessed, and broke it, and gave it to them, and said, 'Take; this is my body.' And he took a cup, and when he had given thanks he gave it to them, and they all drank of it. And he said to them, 'This is my blood of the covenant, which is poured out for many'" (Mark 14:22-24).

For the special celebration of Holy Communion on Maundy Thursday, you might prepare a scarlet pall and veils appliquéd or embroidered with the Jerusalem cross to symbolize the wounds of Christ. The bands at the ends of the arms of the cross stand for the four corners of the earth; Christ suffered death for all people.

The pall, a seven-inch square of stiffened linen, is placed over the wine chalice. You can leave it plain or embroider it with the cross, stiffening it with cardboard or Plexiglas.

The corporal, a 20-inch napkin upon which the communion vessels rest, can be cut from scarlet linen and embroidered.

The chalice veil, usually 30 or 36 inches square, covers the pall and chalice after the Eucharist.

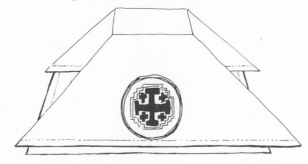

Materials

If chalice is less than 8 inches high: 1 yard scarlet linen, 45 inches wide.

If chalice is more than 8 inches high: 1 yard scarlet linen, 60 inches wide *or* 1 1/2 yards scarlet linen, 45 inches wide.

black fabric
1 piece off-white linen or woven fabric, 5 x 5 inches
black embroidery floss
black, off-white, scarlet thread
fusible webbing
1 piece cardboard or Plexiglas, 7 x 7 inches

Directions

Preparation. Make a pattern for the chalice veil: To determine the size of the finished chalice veil, set a seven-inch square of cardboard on top of the chalice. Measure the length from the altar surface to the cardboard, across the cardboard and down the other side to the altar surface. The total length is the measurement across the square veil after you have hemmed it.

Trace the Jerusalem cross pattern on paper.

Cutting. *Chalice veil*: Cut a square piece of scarlet linen, following the measurements determined (above). Be sure to add 1/4 inch all around to allow for the rolled hems.

Using the pattern, cut the Jerusalem cross from black fabric and fusible webbing.

Corporal: Cut a square of scarlet linen, 20 5/8 x 20 5/8 inches.

Pall: Cut two squares of scarlet linen, each eight inches square.

Construction. *Chalice veil*: Prepare the chalice veil with rolled hems before appliquéing it.

Center the Jerusalem cross in the square of off-white linen. Fuse it in place and machine appliqué the raw edges with black thread. Then set the machine to a straight stitch and sew lines around the crosses to make a border unifying them. Press the back of the appliqué to straighten the stitches.

Following the pattern cut a circle around the appliqué from the off-white linen. Position the circle on the scarlet background fabric. Hand baste, then machine appliqué with off-white thread. Press the appliqué on the back.

Corporal: Hem the square of scarlet linen to a finished size of 20 inches. You may embroider the Jerusalem cross on the fabric.

Pall: Using a 1/2-inch seam allowance, stitch the two squares, right sides together, around three sides. Turn the right side out to make an envelope. You may embroider the Jerusalem cross in the center of the pall.

Insert a seven inch square of cardboard or Plexiglas, and stitch the open end closed.

CROWN OF THORNS STOLE

*"And the soldiers led him away . . . and they
clothed him in a purple cloak, and plaiting a
crown of thorns they put it on him. And they
began to salute him, 'Hail, King of the Jews!' "
(Mark 15:16-18).*

Using angular, pointed, and diagonal design elements, you can create a vestment that recalls Jesus'
suffering and agony. Use reds, purples, greys, and
blacks for the stole's composition, leaving out light
colors. The contrasts of colors should be sharp for
easy reading but low-key in tone.

Materials
2 pieces scarlet fabric, each 60 x 10 inches
2 pieces scarlet lining fabric, each 60 x 10 inches
1 2/3 yards medium weight interfacing, 18 inches
  wide
fusible webbing
red, purple, grey, black fabrics
scarlet, red, purple, grey, black thread

Directions
Preparation. Prepare a stole pattern (page 9).
Enlarge the thorns and *INRI* pattern to four
times its size.
Cutting. Cut the basic stole pattern from the
scarlet fabric.

Cut two sets of letters for *INRI* out of black
fabric, with fusible webbing.

Cut the thorn patterns from black, grey, red, and purple fabrics, each with fusible webbing.

Construction. Position the letters *INRI* on the stole. (You may want to position the letters on a piece of purple fabric and then inset that fabric into the stole.) Fuse them in place and machine appliqué with black thread.

Position the fabrics cut in thorn shapes on the stole pieces. Use your sense of design to create a pattern that is pleasing. Fuse them in place, and machine appliqué with matching threads.

You may wish to add bands of fabric above and below the *INRI* letters, or machine couch black embroidery floss lines across the stole pieces.

Stitch the stole fronts together at the center back seam. Press the seam open. Interface and line the stole.

GOOD FRIDAY

"So they took Jesus, and he went out, bearing his own cross, to the place called the place of the skull, which is called in Hebrew Golgotha. There they crucified him" (John 19:17-18).

Near the end of the Maundy Thursday service, your congregation may strip the worship setting to prepare it for Good Friday. The most somber day of the church year, Good Friday is a day of serious reflection and prayer at the foot of the cross. The chancel is left bare until it is dressed for Easter.

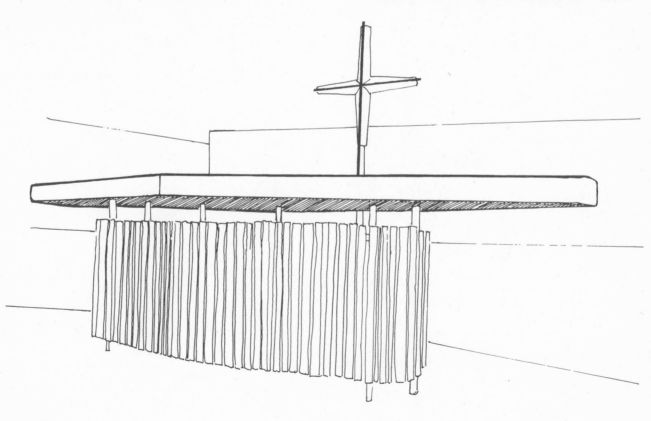

The Easter Season

Alleluia! Alleluia! Christ is risen! Christ is risen indeed!

The colors of the season are white and gold, the whites of the other high festivals with an additional "crown" of gold to give prominence to the most important season of the church year.

Easter whites, when contrasted with the barrenness of the stripped altar of Good Friday, provide the greatest visual change experienced during the church year and highlight this high point of the yearly cycle.

VIGIL OF EASTER BANNERS

The Vigil of Easter is a dramatic crossing from Lent to Easter, from death to life. Through the sacraments of God's saving grace, we move through the dark portal to participate in Christ's rising and our own salvation. The service begins in the darkness; the sanctuary is gradually lit with fire and candles that later give way to full illumination. The elements of fire, light, water, bread, and wine highlight the services.

You may feel that using pictorial symbols for the services would be redundant because the actual symbols of fire, candles, water, bread, and wine are used. However, if your sanctuary provides a unique place to position banners, you may prepare these banners which highlight the themes of the vigil.

Use your creativity in constructing these banners: Make them square, centering the symbol, or make them long and thin, with the symbol near the bottom. Consider the space available in the sanctuary and make the banners to fit.

See page 9 for instructions on assembling banners.

59

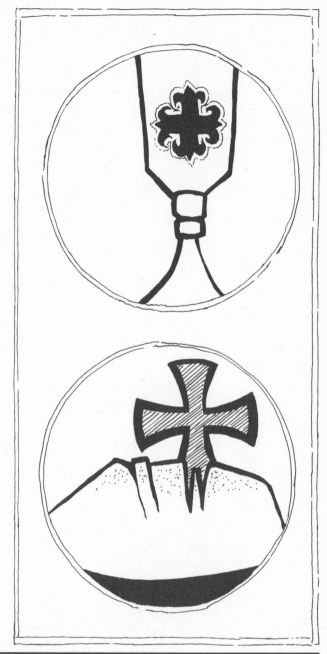

CROSS AND CROWN PULPIT/LECTERN CLOTH

"Be faithful unto death, and I will give you the crown of life" (Revelation 2:10).

A patchwork of crosses and crowns appliquéd to blocks of white and gold fabric compliments the Sun of Righteousness altar cloths, extending the festival's colors to the pulpit and/or lectern.

Size

The finished size for the drop is 13 x 19 inches. The depth must be added.

Materials

3 pieces gold corduroy, 7 x 7 inches
3 pieces white brushed corduroy, 7 x 7 inches
1/8 yard each gold satin, white satin
1/2 yard white lining fabric, 45 inches wide
gold, white embroidery floss
gold, white thread
1/2 yard fusible webbing
1 piece quilt batting, 14 x 20 inches

Directions

Preparation. Trace the cross and crown patterns on paper.

Cutting. Cut three crowns from gold satin and three crosses from white satin, each with fusible webbing.

Construction. Center a crown in each white corduroy square. Fuse them in place, and machine appliqué with gold thread.

Center a cross in each gold corduroy square. Fuse them in place, and machine appliqué with white thread.

Using a 1/2-inch seam allowance, stitch the squares together. Alternate the squares to form a checkerboard pattern as shown in the illustration.

Position the piece of quilt batting on the back of the hanging. Quilt the layers together by hand, stitching along the seam lines and around the appliquéd shapes. Then, moving your stitching line 3/4 inch away from the first stitching line, stitch again inside the borders of the squares and around the appliqués.

Line the cloth with white fabric and add the needed drop to the hanging to suspend it from the pulpit or lectern bookrest.

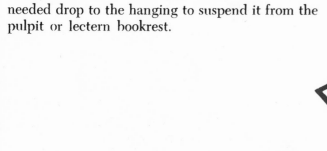

CROSS OF VICTORY STOLE

"I shall not die, but I shall live, and recount the deeds of the Lord. The Lord has chastened me sorely, but he has not given me over to death. Open to me the gates of righteousness, that I may enter through them and give thanks to the Lord" (Psalm 118:17-19).

Use a bright, white, high quality fabric with rich texture and light sheen.

Materials

1 2/3 yards white fabric, 45 inches wide
1 2/3 yards white lining fabric, 45 inches wide
1 2/3 yards interfacing, 18 inches wide
black, orange, bright pink heavy yarn
scraps of bright gold, hot pink fabrics
fusible webbing
black, orange, white, pink thread

Directions

Preparation. Prepare the shaped stole pattern (page 9). Trace the crown and circle patterns on paper.

Cutting. Using the shaped stole pattern, cut the stole fronts from the white fabric.

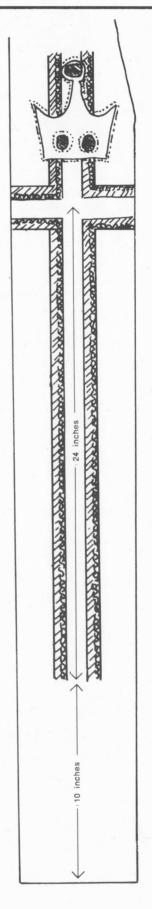

black yarn

pink yarn

orange yarn

24 inches

10 inches

Cut two crowns from bright gold fabric and fusible webbing.

Cut six circles from hot pink fabric and fusible webbing.

Construction. With a machine stitch, run a line of stay-stitching along the raw edges of the stole fronts to keep the weave from unraveling while doing the hand embroidery.

Mark the cross on each stole front with a dressmaker's marker according to the diagram.

Hand couch each color of yarn in place according to the diagram.

Position three pink circles on each crown as indicated in the diagram. Fuse them in place and machine appliqué with pink thread.

Position a gold crown at the top of each cross. Fuse them in place, and machine appliqué with gold thread.

Press the appliqués on the back side. Seam the stole fronts together at the center back. Finish with interfacing and lining.

RESURRECTION STOLE

"I am the resurrection and the life" (John 11:25).

This stole design shows the butterfly, a popular symbol for resurrection. For the Easter season you could repeat the butterfly symbol on a stole, making a progression of colors from pale grey, gold, yellow, to off-white. Crown it with a bright, white butterfly marked with the cross.

Materials

2 pieces white brushed corduroy, each 60 x 10 inches

2 pieces white lining fabric, each 60 x 10 inches

1 2/3 yards medium-weight interfacing, 18 inches wide

1/8 yard each pale grey, gold, yellow, off-white, white cottons.

3/4 yard fusible webbing

dark grey, white thread

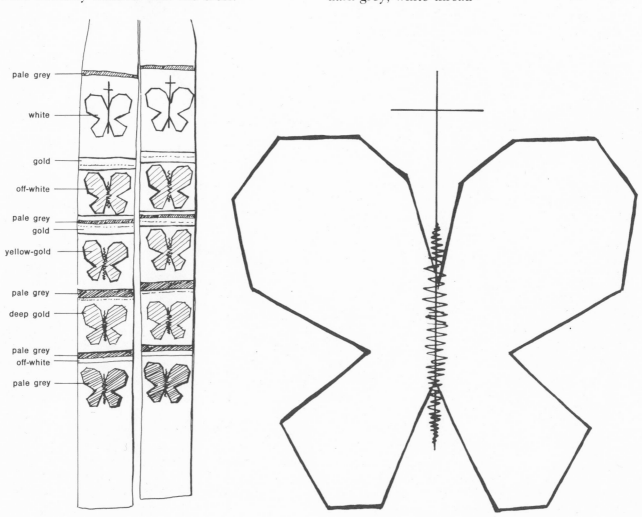

Directions

Preparation. Prepare the shaped stole pattern. Trace the butterfly pattern on paper.

Cutting. Cut two butterflies, each with fusible webbing, out of each of the following: pale grey, gold, yellow, off-white, white cotton.

Using the pattern, cut the stole pieces from the white fabric.

Cut bands which will be used to separate the parts of the progression. Use the diagram as a guide for width and color.

Construction. Position five butterflies on each stole front (bottom to top: grey, gold, yellow, off-white, white). Fuse them in place, and machine appliqué with grey thread. Sew through the middle of the butterfly to create its body, changing the zigzag width to define the shape.

Position the color bands according to the diagram, pin them in place, and zigzag along raw edges with grey thread. Add detail by stitching straight lines across the bands.

Press the appliqués on the back. Stitch the stole fronts together at the back neck seam, and press the seam open. Finish the stole with interfacing and lining.

AGNUS DEI BANNER

This is the time for the most dramatic banner-making. The *Agnus Dei*, or Lamb of God, is the victorious lamb, pictured with the banner of the cross of resurrection. Churches with traditional worship centers would find this banner design appropriate. The design could be made in multiples and carried by many on a great number of small banners or reproduced on one large banner, carried by one in a procession and set in a holder near the altar for the service.

See page 9 for instructions on enlarging the Agnus Dei design to fit your chosen banner size. Then use your imagination for determining size, fabric, and color.

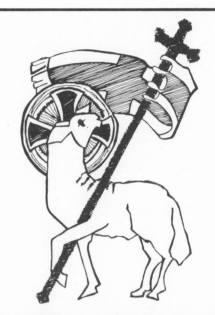

LETTERED BANNER

A more contemporary banner, the lettered appliqué banner, could be carried into the sanctuary in sections and hung on hooks already set into the walls. The visual assembling of the graphic message before the eyes of the congregation on each Sunday of the Easter season gives drama and accent to the season.

Since the walls of each worship setting differ vastly, design instructions are not included. This is your chance to create the drama for your congregation, fitting the banners to your particular situation. See page 9 for instructions on making letter patterns. The banner design presents great possibilities for creative use of texture and color.

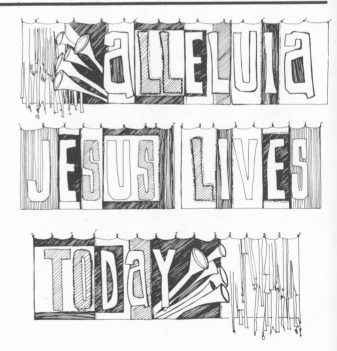

SUN OF RIGHTEOUSNESS ALTAR CLOTH

"And very early on the first day of the week they went to the tomb when the sun had risen . . . And entering the tomb, they saw a young man sitting on the right side, dressed in a white robe; and they were amazed. And he said to them, 'Do not be amazed; you seek Jesus of Nazareth, who was crucified. He has risen, he is not here'" (Mark 16:2, 5-6).

The Sun of Righteousness Altar Cloth celebrates that the Son has risen. To make the cloth, refer to page 31. (You may already have used the cloth for Christmas.) You may want to double the sun symbol for a bigger effect.

THE ASCENSION OF OUR LORD CLOTHS

"As they were looking on, he was lifted up, and a cloud took him out of their sight" (Acts 1:9).

This is another occasion to use the white banded cloths and vestments suggested for The Transfiguration of Our Lord during the Christmas Cycle. Refer to Chapter 4 for the instructions (page 47).

SPIRIT OF THE LORD ALTAR CLOTH

"And there appeared to them tongues as of fire, distributed and resting on each one of them. And they were all filled with the Holy Spirit" (Acts 2:3-4).

The Day of Pentecost, the birthday of the church, spurs Christ's followers into action, the fire of the Holy Spirit lighting the spirit of love, enthusiasm, and dedication to the spreading of the Gospel. We celebrate the festival with bright red. Red suggests love, the passion of the heart, and the zeal inspired by Pentecost. The descending dove, still the most easily recognized symbol for the Spirit of the Lord, hovers above the flame.

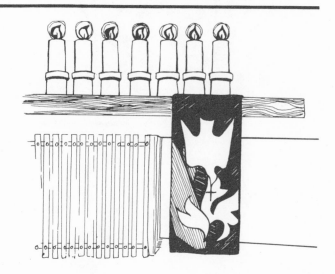

We are reminded that the Holy Spirit breathes life into the church of Christ, giving workers in the church purpose and directions.

You could culminate the Easter Cycle with these red paraments and vestments. The white dove on a red background makes a dynamic focal point on an altar hanging or chasuble.

Size

This project gives instructions for making a single altar cloth drop with a finished size of 14 x 34 inches. The depth must be added.

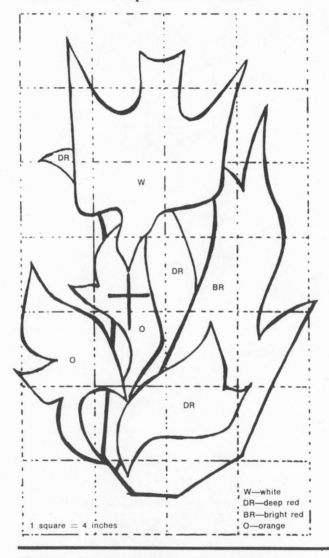

W—white
DR—deep red
BR—bright red
O—orange

1 square = 4 inches

SPIRIT OF THE LORD CHASUBLE

"Receive the Holy Spirit. If you forgive the sins of any, they are forgiven; if you retain the sins of any, they are retained" (John 20:22-23).

Use the same procedure for this chasuble as was suggested for the altar cloth.

Materials

1 piece red velveteen, corduroy, or trigger, 16 x 34 inches
1 piece heavyweight interfacing, 14 x 32 inches
1 piece lining fabric, 16 x 34 inches
°1/2 yard white heavy broadcloth or white satin
°1/2 yard orange broadcloth or satin
°1/2 yard fusible webbing
°1 yard each deep red and bright red cotton fabric
°red, white thread

Directions

Preparation. Enlarge the dove and flames pattern as specified. Make two copies of the enlarged pattern, one for a master copy and one to cut apart to use as a pattern when cutting the appliqué pieces from fabric. Make a third copy of the pattern for the two large flames which tuck behind the smaller ones.

Cutting. Cut the pattern pieces from the fabrics, following the color key. The two large flames are cut as complete units, and the smaller flames are placed on top of the larger flames. However, the flame pieces are cut out to fit around the dove's head like a jigsaw puzzle. This avoids a distracting ridge behind the dove.

Cut a layer of fusible webbing in the dove shape.

Construction. Position the two large flame pieces on the red background and arrange the dove so its head fits into its niche. Pin the flames in place, then fuse the dove onto the red background. Baste around the flames with a running stitch 1/4 inch from the raw edges. Machine appliqué around the raw edges of the flames with red thread.

Then arrange the three small flames over the large flames, hand baste, and machine appliqué the edges with red thread. Finally, machine appliqué around the dove using white thread.

Stitch the white cross on the flame with a wide, close zigzag stitch. Press the appliqué on the back side. Interface and line the cloth, adding the depth needed to suspend the cloth in front of the altar.

Materials

3 1/2 yards red velveteen, corduroy, or trigger, 52 inches wide

---

° If both the Spirit of the Lord altar cloth and the Spirit of the Lord chasuble are made, it is not necessary to duplicate these materials. For example, only ½ yard of orange broadcloth provides enough material for both pieces.

°1/2 yard white heavy broadcloth or white satin
°1/2 yard orange broadcloth
°1/2 yard fusible webbing
°1 yard each deep red and bright red cotton fabric
°red, white thread
8 yards deep red bias tape

Directions

Preparation. Prepare the long chasuble pattern (page 8). Enlarge the flame and dove pattern from the Day of Pentecost altar cloth as specified.

Cutting. Using the long chasuble pattern, cut the chasuble pieces from the red velveteen, corduroy, or trigger. To do this, open the width out to its 52 inches and fold the entire length in half.

Cut out the dove and flame pieces from the fabrics, following the color key. The two large flames are cut as complete units, and the smaller flames are placed on top of the larger flames. However, the flames pieces are cut out to fit around the dove's head like a jigsaw puzzle. This avoids a distracting ridge behind the dove.

Cut a layer of fusible webbing in the dove shape.

Construction. Seam center back and center front of the chasuble. Press the seams open.

The appliqué can be affixed either to the back or to the front of the chasuble. Position the two large flame pieces on the red background and arrange the dove so its head fits into the niche. Pin the flames in place, then fuse the dove onto the red background. Baste around the flames with a running stitch 1/4 inch from the raw edge. Machine appliqué around the raw edges of the flames with red thread.

Then arrange the three small flames over the large flames, hand baste, and machine appliqué the edges with red thread. Finally, machine appliqué around the dove using white thread.

Stitch the white cross on the flame with a wide, close, zigzag stitch. Press the appliqué on the back side.

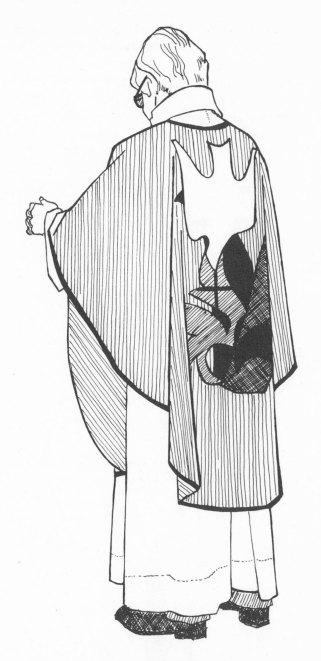

Sew the chasuble front and back together at the shoulder seams. Press the seams open. Trim the hem and neck edges with the bias tape.

NIKA STOLE

These four letters spell out an abbreviation for the words, "Victory over death." Stitched in a red fabric, the stole carries the Easter theme of victory over death into The Day of Pentecost.

Materials
1 1/2 yards red woven fabric
1/2 yard fusible webbing
scraps white, orange, pink, dark purple, light purple cottons or satins
2 purchased butterfly appliqués
red thread
2 pieces lining fabric, 60 x 10 inches
2 pieces interfacing, 60 x 10 inches

Directions
Preparation. Prepare a stole pattern (page 9).

Prepare patterns for the letters *NIKA* (see page 9). The letters should be one inch shorter than the stole is wide.

Cutting. Using the stole pattern, cut the stole pieces from the red woven fabric.

Cut two pieces of pink fabric, 7 x 5 1/2 inches.

Cut two of each of the letters from the following colors: dark purple *A*, white *K*, orange *I*, light purple *N*, each with fusible webbing.

Construction. Place one of the pink pieces on each stole front, 18 inches from the center back seam. Machine appliqué the raw edges with red thread.

Apply the butterfly appliqués, centered in the pink sections. Add strips of red and purple fabrics above and below the butterflies on the pink fabric. Machine appliqué with red thread.

Position the letters on the stole fronts (see illustration). Fuse them in place and machine appliqué with red thread.

Add dark purple strips below the lettering. Machine appliqué with red thread.

Sew the stole fronts together at the back neck seam. Press the seam open and the appliqués on the back side. Interface and line the stole.

CRUSADER CROSS STOLE

The most universal symbol of Christianity, the cross stands for the story of salvation and the work of the church. Sometimes we say that the vertical line of the cross represents God reaching down to humanity while the horizontal arm represents people reaching out to each other in response to what God has done. The Crusader cross, an emblem of Pentecost, extends its four crossed arms to the four corners of the earth. Emblazoned on the stole, it tells of the love Christ has for all people and the love people have for each other because of Christ.

Materials

You can fashion this liturgical stole from scraps and patches of fabrics. Combine a variety of rich textures, velveteens with satins, corduroys with metallics, perhaps a little bright-colored felt.

Directions

Preparation. Trace the cross pattern on paper.

Make a pattern for the upper stole fronts by measuring 40 inches from the bottom of the full-size stole pattern (page 9). From that point to the back neck seam becomes the upper stole front pattern.

Cutting. Cut six pieces (7 x 9 inches) from one color and four from another color fabric. Cut six crosses from a color contrasting the six rectangles and four crosses from a color contrasting the four rectangles, each with fusible webbing.

Cut the upper stole fronts from the same fabric as the four rectangles.

Construction. Center a cross in a contrasting colored rectangle. Fuse it in place and machine appliqué using matching thread. Repeat this for all 10 rectangles.

Sew five rectangles together, alternating colors and using a 1/2-inch seam allowance. Sew the resulting band to the upper stole front. Repeat this for the other side of the stole.

Sew the stole fronts together at the back neck seam. Press all seams open and all appliqués on the back side. Interface and line the stole.

VENI, CREATOR SPIRITUS STOLE

Experiment with lettering on a cowled stole (page 9) by decorating two 7 x 55 inch strips with letters. Tuck chunks of contrasting colors between letters and under letters. Fill openings of each *o, p,* and *a.* This is your chance for rich stitching and rich coloring. Use hot pinks, purples, golds, yellow-golds, hot oranges, and reds. Use high contrasts of light and dark. The result should reflect the reverberating zeal of Pentecost!

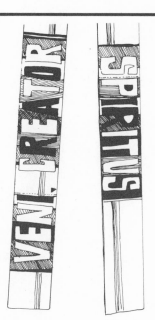

Chapter 6

THE TIME OF THE CHURCH

Symbols for the first half of the church year center around God's creation and the story of salvation. The designs on the worship cloths reflect the mysteries of God, the work of the Father, Son, and Holy Spirit in our lives. During the Pentecost season, a new family of symbols can be utilized. The long Season after Pentecost is The Time of the Church—a time to respond to God's grace, to look toward spiritual growth, and to explore the teachings of Christ.

Some of the most well-known Pentecost symbols are vines, branches bearing fruit, wheat, grapes, birds, fish, water, bread, and wine. We see ourselves as branches bearing fruit, birds feeding upon the food of the Scriptures, participants in the sacraments, workers in the field, and messengers of the gospel.

As you begin The Time of the Church, put away all items from the Easter Cycle so that you get another fresh beginning. The season is a long one and to keep it fresh and invigorating for worshipers, you can give the sanctuary variety through banners and several sets of paraments. A single altar cloth that hangs during the entire season of 20-some Sundays may become tedious. Worshipers may appreciate a change and find themselves renewed by a change of worship cloths.

The color for the Sundays after Pentecost is green. You may use the same green cloths as for the Season of Epiphany. Some additional green cloths, adding the deeper, more mature greens of late summer and fall harvest might also be used during this long season. Deepening the greens may symbolize the deepening and maturing of the Christian life and indicate the harvest of the fruits of the Spirit. Green depicts life and rebirth.

In the following pages you will find a number of possibilities for paraments, vestments, and banners for the many Sundays after Pentecost. This series relates to the Gospels that are read during the season. You might make several sets of paraments, changing them as the season progresses.

The designs are accompanied by the scripture texts from which they are drawn. If you wish to make up your own designs, refer to the appointed lessons. There is much to be learned and much to teach through visual images.

The designs are also accompanied by illustrations you can enlarge to fit the cloth you are making. Use the methods of enlargement described in Chapter 3. Better yet, change the designs around a bit, or make up your own. The designs are not accompanied by step-by-step procedures for making the items; it is intended that you explore the possibilities.

With some designs in this chapter is a reference to a similar design in Chapter 4 or 5. By reading the instructions for the earlier design, you may get a sense of what must be done for this design—both materials and technique.

PARABLE OF THE SOWER ALTAR AND PULPIT/LECTERN CLOTHS AND STOLE

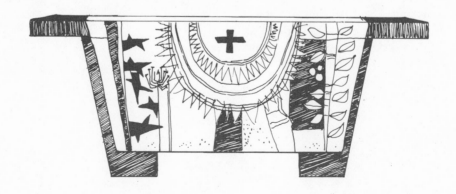

"And he told them many things in parables, saying: 'A sower went out to sow. And as he sowed, some seeds fell along the path . . . Other seeds fell on rocky ground . . . Other seeds fell on good soil and brought forth grain, some a hundredfold, some sixty, some thirty'" (Matthew 13:3-8).

These altar, pulpit, and lectern cloths illustrate the parable of the good and poor soils upon which the seeds are sown. Some of the patterns for the appliqué were borrowed from previous chapters (thorns on page 58, sun on page 32) and a few more are included here. You will need to adapt the pattern to fit the dimensions of your altar, pulpit, or lectern.

See pages 17 and 31 for instructions on constructing and appliquéing an altar cloth. See page 20 for instructions for the pulpit/lectern cloth.

For color, you might explore the warm color ranges, appliquéing oranges, browns, greys, and yellows on green backgrounds. For an interesting background, patch together several shades of green.

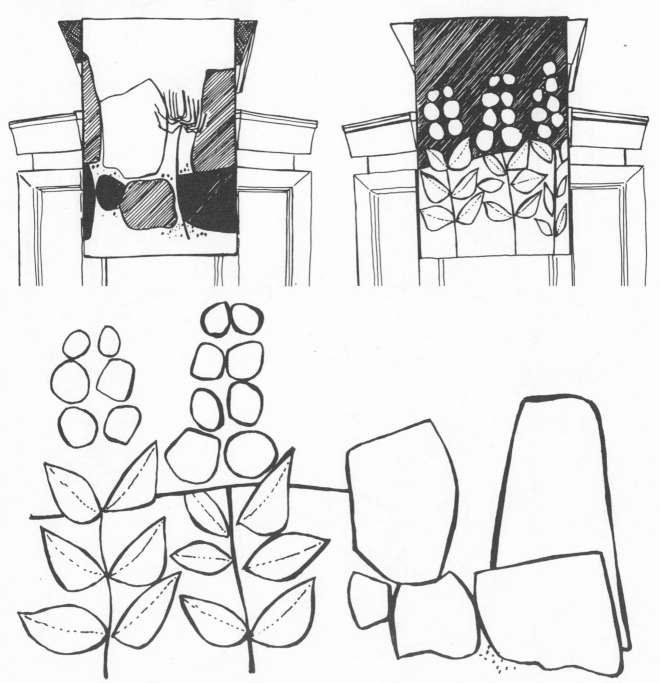

Other images from the parable can be attached to the pastor's stole. Birds that ate the seed can be pictured on one side while the wheat that grew from the seed founded in firm soil can be seen on the other side. The combination of images on the altar cloth, pulpit cloth, lectern cloth, and stole tell the story of how the gospel is received by God's people.

Actual-size appliqué patterns for the stole are given here and on page 76. See page 9 for stole patterns. See page 11 for appliqué instructions and stole construction techniques.

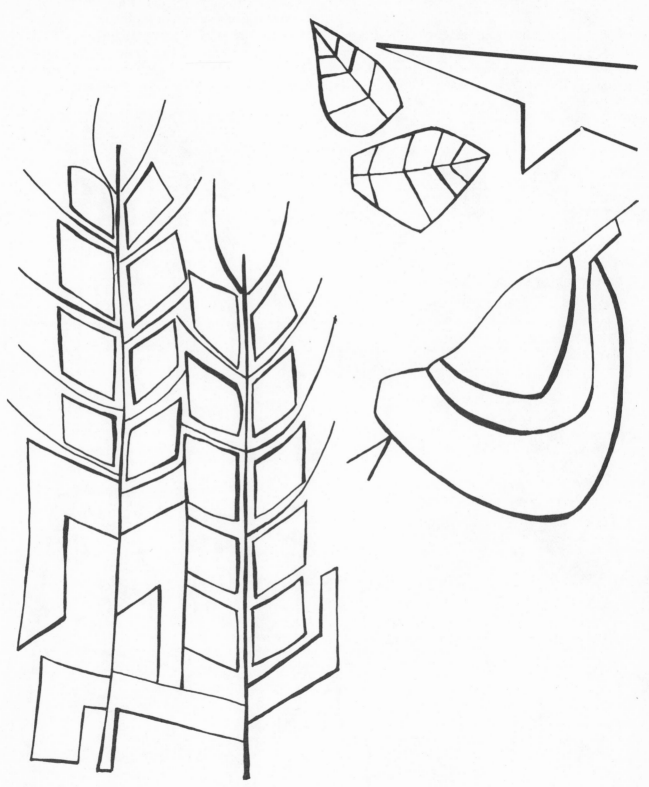

THE HOLY TRINITY BANNER

"And Jesus came and said to them, 'All authority in heaven and on earth has been given to me. Go therefore and make disciples of all nations, baptizing them in the name of the Father and of the Son and of the Holy Spirit'" (Matthew 28:18-19).

For The Holy Trinity (First Sunday after Pentecost), the color is white. This festival ushers God's people into the long Season after Pentecost. It emphasizes the presence of the triune God during this time of growth in the Christian church.

Celebrate with symbols of the Trinity. Among the most easily recognized symbols for the triune God are interlocking circles or triangles or combinations of both. A banner may be all you need to add to the white paraments and vestments you already have for white Sundays.

Circles and triangles are easy to design for use on the banner. Draw them on paper and then enlarge them to fit the banner size you have chosen. Then appliqué the designs in place. See page 9 for instructions on banner construction and design.

THE HOLY TRINITY CHASUBLE

For this chasuble, which features three crosses, refer to Chapter 3 (page 8) for the basic chasuble pattern. See page 61 for the cross design and directions for the appliqué. See page 15 for directions for construction of the chasuble. Appliqué the crosses on the back or front of the chasuble and trim the appliqués with gold braids or other ornamentation.

Three crosses, three circles, and a triangle symbolize the union of the Father, Son, and Holy Spirit. A fourth similar element such as the radiating cross at the top of the chasuble may suggest the church at large, a living testimony to the work of the triune God. You may wish to invent some symbols of your own for appliqué that are meaningful to your particular congregation.

FISH AND LOAVES PULPIT/LECTERN CLOTH AND STOLE

"Then he ordered the crowds to sit down on the grass; and taking the five loaves and the two fish he looked up to heaven, and blessed, and broke and gave the loaves to the disciples, and the disciples gave them to the crowds" (Matthew 14:19).

This lesson also supplies images for appliqué. Combine the fish and loaves in mirror images for the pulpit and lectern.

See page 11 for construction and appliqué techniques.

The same symbols that appear on the pulpit and lectern multiply visually if appliquéd to the pastor's stole. This may be a good way to illustrate the miracle of the multiplication of the fish and loaves during the feeding of the 5000. Actual-size patterns for the stole appliqués are given.

See pages 11 and 15 for instructions on stole construction and appliqué.

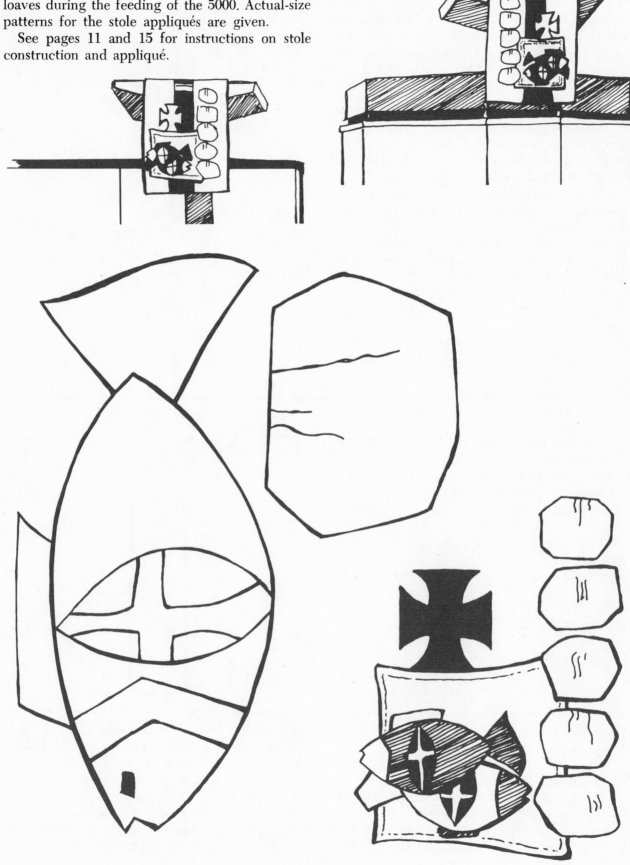

PEOPLE OF GOD ALTAR AND PULPIT/LECTERN CLOTHS

"I am the living bread which came down from heaven; if any one eats of this bread, he will live for ever" (John 6:51).

The dove has long been a symbol for the faithful Christian. Here is a great opportunity to illustrate the feeding of those who hunger for the teachings of Christ and for his body and blood in Holy Communion. The designs demonstrate repetition of a singular motif. Doves are grouped in patterns, to symbolize the faithful followers of Jesus Christ eagerly communing at his table.

Color the basic cloths in green and appliqué grey or white doves on the surfaces. Add purples and browns or tans for the grape and wheat motifs. See pages 17 and 31 for altar cloth construction directions. See page 20 for pulpit/lectern cloth construction directions.

PEOPLE OF GOD STOLE

A stole might be appliquéd with the dove, wheat, and grape motifs. Actual-size patterns suitable for a stole printed with the chasuble instructions on the next page and on page 72. See page 9 for stole patterns. See page 15 for instructions for sewing a stole.

PEOPLE OF GOD CHASUBLE

Repeat the dove, wheat, grapes motifs again and again on the front or back of the chasuble. Add the *IHS* to symbolize Jesus Christ, the Bread of heaven. Use the long chasuble pattern (page 8). See page 15 for instructions for appliquéing and constructing a chasuble.

FLOWERING VINE ALTAR AND PULPIT/LECTERN CLOTHS

"I am the vine, you are the branches. He who abides in me, and I in him, he it is that bears much fruit, for apart from me you can do nothing" (John 15:4-5).

The flowering vine is a symbol of Christ's living church. The vine symbol might be repeated on all chancel furnishings.

The shapes of the long hangings give variety to the previously short hangings. The background fabrics are stripes of two shades of green. The altar cloths might hang nearly to the floor, with the pulpit and lectern cloths of equal length.

Enlarge the vine and branches pattern so that it stretches the length of the cloths.

See page 17 for instructions on altar cloth construction. See page 20 for pulpit/lectern cloth instructions.

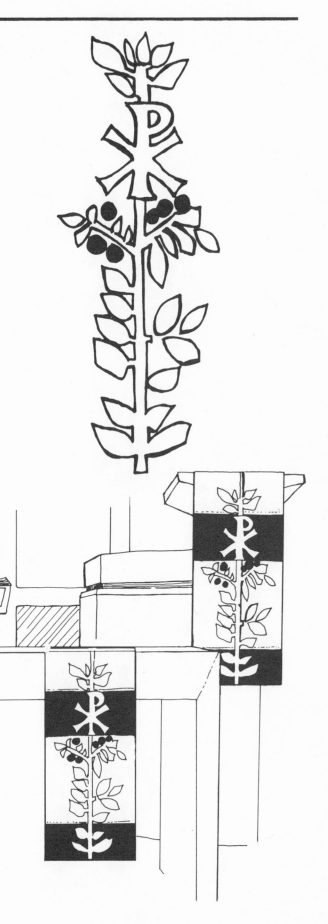

FLOWERING VINE CHASUBLE

Create a festive green chasuble, and freely apply leaves and a symbol for Jesus Christ at the center back.

You might bend the branches and leaves so they follow the hem of the chasuble. Then add the Chi-Rho, a symbol for Jesus Christ (page 47). This design idea is illustrated. Or, you might use the same vine and branches pattern as the altar cloth, and run it up the center front of the chasuble.

See page 8 for chasuble patterns. (The illustration shows the short chasuble.) See page 11 for instructions on appliquéing and constructing a chasuble.

FRUITS OF THE SPIRIT STOLE

"But the fruit of the Spirit is love, joy, peace, patience, kindness, goodness, faithfulness, gentleness, self-control" (Galatians 5:22-23).

Round out the green Sundays after Pentecost with symbols for the fruits of the Spirit. In early America, a symbol was developed for each of these characteristics of the Christian:

love—carnation or heart
joy—wild rose
peace—olive branch

patience—ox
kindness—cherry
goodness—orange

faithfulness—stork
gentleness—lamb

self-control—bridle

Find simple line drawings which might serve as patterns for these symbols. Then appliqué each symbol on a square of green fabric. Because there are nine fruits, you might want to add a symbol for the Spirit (page 66). Appliqué that on a tenth square. Sew these squares together (five on a side) to form the lower stole fronts. Add the upper stole fronts to complete this Fruits of the Spirit stole.

See page 40 for cutting, appliqué, and construction instructions for this type of stole. See page 9 for stole patterns.

CHRIST THE KING BANNER

"He has delivered us from the dominion of darkness and transferred us to the kingdom of his beloved Son, in whom we have redemption, the forgiveness of sins" (Colossians 1:13-14).

The Holy Trinity signals the beginning of The Time of the Church while Christ the King signals its end. The church year is completed with the festival of Christ the King.

Cover the furnishings in white as for the other festivals of our Lord.

A white banner can mark the celebration of Christ's redemption and our forgiveness. Decorate the banner with the kingly symbols of cross and crown. Use regal colors—white, gold, royal blue, purple, and red.

See page 36 for the symbol patterns. See page 9 for banner construction directions.

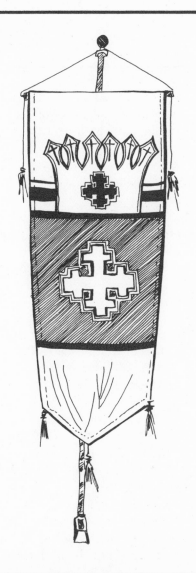

CHRIST THE KING CHASUBLE

Make the chasuble a stunning patchwork of crosses and crowns.

Cut the crosses and crowns from various gold fabrics and appliqué them to white fabric squares. Sew the squares together in the chasuble shape.

See page 8 for chasuble patterns. See page 40 for instructions on assembling and appliquéing squares. See page 15 for chasuble construction information.

GLOSSARY

Alb: A white or off-white full-length vestment with sleeves, worn by all ranks of ministers.

Altar: The table on which Holy Communion is celebrated.

Appliqué: A cut-out decoration fastened to a larger piece of material (i.e., banner, vestment, or parament).

Banner: A decorated fabric hanging which is carried in processions or used as a wall hanging.

Cassock: A full-length black robe worn under the surplice by clergy, choir, musicians, and acolytes.

Chalice: The cup used to contain the wine in Holy Communion.

Chasuble: A poncho-like garment worn over the alb by the presiding minister as the principal vestment at the celebration of Holy Communion.

Church year: A representation of the life of Christ in a yearly pattern with two centers—the Christmas and Easter events.

Cincture: A belt of fabric, leather, or rope worn around the waist of an alb or cassock.

Corporal: A square of white linen placed on the center of the altar, on which sacramental vessels are placed.

Couching: Embroidering with laid threads fastened by small stitches at regular intervals.

Cowled stole: A stole with cording at chest height which can be put behind the neck to form a hood effect.

Depth: The section of a parament which lays over the top of the altar or over the bookrest of the pulpit or lectern.

Drop: The decorated section of a parament which hangs in front of the altar, pulpit, or lectern.

Embroidery: The forming of decorative designs with hand or machine needlework.

Eucharist: The service of Holy Communion.

Font: The basin which holds water for Holy Baptism.

Frontal: A parament, usually in the liturgical color, which covers the entire front of the altar.

Frontlet: A narrow band in the liturgical color which extends across the top of the front of an altar. Also called a superfrontal.

Fusible webbing: A thin, webbed material which, when placed between two layers of fabric and then pressed with a hot iron, bonds the two fabric pieces together.

Grain: The direction of threads in a piece of fabric.

Interfacing: A firm cloth shaped and sewn between the facing and outside of a garment for stiffening and shape retention.

Lectern: A reading stand from which scripture lessons are read.

Lesson: A passage from the Scriptures read in a worship service.

Lining: The material used to line the inner surface of something.

Pall: A linen-covered square used to cover the chalice during Holy Communion.

Paraments: The general name for cloth hangings in the liturgical colors used on the altar, pulpit, and lectern.

Pulpit: A raised reading desk from which the sermon is delivered.

Satin stitch: An embroidery stitch nearly alike on both sides and worked so closely as to resemble satin.

Seam allowance: The width of fabric beyond the seam line, not including the garment area.

Shaped stole: A stole with a shaped neck.

Slipstitch: A concealed stitch for sewing folded edges made by alternately running the needle inside the fold and picking up a thread or two from the body of the article.

Stole: A scarf of fabric in the liturgical color worn over the shoulders by ordained ministers.

Superfrontal: A band of fabric that extends across the front of the altar.

Surplice: A white vestment of various lengths worn over the cassock by ministers of the service.

Veil: A cloth covering for sacramental vessels used in the celebration of Holy Communion.

Vestments: The outer garments worn by ministers during worship services.

Whipstitch: A shallow overcasting stitch.

Zigzag stitch: A machine stitch having short, sharp turns or angles.